WORLD
HISTORY

Ancient History, United States History, European, Native American, Russian, Chinese, Asian, Indian and Australian History, Wars including World War I and II [4th Edition]

This document aims to provide exact and reliable information in regards to the topics and issues covered. The publication is sold with the idea that the publisher is not required to render accounting, officially permitted, or otherwise, qualified services. If advice is necessary, legal or professional, a practiced individual in the profession should be ordered.

- From a Declaration of Principles which was accepted and approved equally by a Committee of the American Bar Association and a Committee of Publishers and Associations.

In no way is it legal to reproduce, duplicate, or transmit any part of this document in either electronic means or in printed format. Recording of this publication is strictly prohibited and any storage of this document is not allowed unless with written permission from the publisher. All rights reserved.

The information provided herein is stated to be truthful and consistent, in that any liability, in terms of inattention or otherwise, by any usage or abuse of any policies, processes, or directions contained within is the solitary and utter responsibility of the recipient reader. Under no circumstances will any legal responsibility or blame be held against the publisher for any reparation, damages, or monetary loss due to the information herein, either directly or indirectly.

Respective authors own all copyrights not held by the publisher.

The information herein is offered for informational purposes solely, and is universal as so. The presentation of the information is without contract or any type of guarantee assurance.

The trademarks that are used are without any consent, and the publication of the trademark is without permission or backing by the trademark owner. All trademarks and brands within this book are for clarifying purposes only and are owned by the owners themselves, not affiliated with this document.

ISBN 978-1-9992202-3-5 (Paperback)
Published by Pluto King Publishing

Table of Contents

Chapter 3– European and Russian History. 72

Introduction

I firstly wish to both sincerely thank you and congratulate you for purchasing: World History, a book that details the history of the entire world, as we know it.

From the earliest periods of humanity to the modern age, history has long fascinated the public. There are countless lessons to be learned from each country and each geographical location. Over the last several thousand years numerous empires and cultures have risen to great heights, only to be brought low, toppled by new civilizations. Each civilization has contributed to various human achievements that we continue to learn from as we progress into the future.

Thank you again for downloading this book, I truly hope you enjoy it. If it does bring you enjoyment please take a moment to leave a review on Amazon. I would greatly appreciate it.

Chapter 1– Ancient History

The ancient world is generally considered to have existed before the 1st century CE. During this time a number of civilizations sprang up around the then known world, many of which stamped a deep mark upon history. This is a period steeped richly in legend and mythology, a time that still captivates and inspires us today. Read on to discover some of the best-known cultures from ancient history.

Ancient Greece

Ancient Greece is perhaps one of the most well known civilizations from this period. Located in Southeast Europe, and known as *Hellas* or *Ellada* in Greek, it largely consisted of the Balkan Peninsula and countless islands scattered across the Mediterranean Sea. Ancient Greece saw the birth of astronomy, Western philosophy, great thinkers, (including Socrates, Aristotle and Plato), pure mathematics, biology, democracy and even the Olympic Games. Ancient Greece was surprisingly much more scientific than what it is often given credit for: Both Democritus and Leucippus put forth their theory of an atomic universe at this time. Via the visually similar Cumaean Greek version of the Greek alphabet, ancient Greece provided the foundations of the later Roman Latin alphabet, which in turn was derived from the Phoenicians who had brought their script based on Egyptian hieroglyphics into the country at the times Archimedes became a pioneer in engineering and physics.

Greece is surrounded by the Mediterranean Sea on three sides and also consists of several clusters of islands grouped together; these include the Cyclades, the Dodecanese, the

Ionians, the island of Crete and the peninsula region called the Peloponnese. All of these areas had their own identities and unique cultures at the time before they were grouped under the umbrella of ancient Greek history.

The geomorphology of the landscape had a deep impact on the culture and identity of ancient Greece, because being surrounded by water – and with little in the way of natural resources on land – it was the sea that provided much of the people's needs. Around eighty percent of Greece is mountainous so as a result the earliest Greeks took to the waves, establishing colonies on the various islands along what is now modern day Turkey and referred to in antiquity as Asia Minor. The ancient Greeks developed a reputation of being accomplished seafarers and as merchants who traded in raw building materials. A people who also saw rise amongst them great architects, people who created some of the most awe-inspiring buildings and monuments in history.

Ancient Greek history is usually divided into several eras. During the Paleolithic era the region was already inhabited by humans, as is indicated by evidence that was found at the Franchthi and the Petralona caves, then, during the Neolithic era (c. 6,000 – 2,900 BCE), Greece established various small permanent settlements and began the domestication of animals as well as establishing the cultivation of grains, notably barley, and wheat. The archaeological record at places such as Sesklo, Thessaly and Macedonia in northern Greece suggests that there was an exodus from Anatolia, which can be seen mostly in the distinct styles of pottery that were found in Neolithic Anatolia. Those who lived in northern Greece were the first farmers in the country, because this area was much more suited to agriculture. Houses here were typically one story high with a single room and a wooden roof.

The Cycladic Civilization (3,200 – 1,100 BCE) developed across the islands that are located in the Aegean Sea, including Delos, Paros and Naxos, and are places that indicate the first signs of continuous human occupation, as here both residential and religious Greek buildings were constructed with stone. The people are known to have relied on trading and fishing to survive because the economy was not advanced enough to support other types of commerce. This era is separated into three sub-periods: the Early Cycladic, the Middle Cycladic and the Late Cycladic Period and within all of these periods there was a progression in complexity in the arts and the construction of buildings. The Middle Cycladic and the Late Cycladic Periods corresponded with the Minoan period, where the two finally combined with no recognizable differences.

The Minoan era (2,700 – 1,500 BCE) began on the island of Crete, which is located to the south of the country's borders. The Minoan civilization flourished, rose and expanded rapidly, and although no one knows exactly how they referred to themselves, the culture was titled as Minoan by the famous archaeologist Sir Arthur Evans. He discovered the Minoan palace of Knossos at the turn of the 20th century, which was named after the renowned ruler of Crete, King Minos.

A writing system, known to the world as Linear A – and one of the earliest – was developed on the island of Minoan Crete and is still yet to be fully deciphered. We also know that the people were skilled ship builders, artists, scientists and formidable fighters. Numerous ancient historians – including Thucydides – name Minos as the first Cretan king to establish a kingdom as a naval power, one that enabled him to conquer and colonize the Cyclades. The archaeological record suggests that the Minoans overused the natural resources of the island and caused deforestation; a process that continued until they were eventually defeated by the Mycenaeans.

The region also experienced one of the largest volcanic eruptions in the last 10,000 years when it occurred at what is now known as Santorini (The Minoan eruption of Thera), somewhere between 1650 – 1550 BCE. The eruption resulted in a massive tsunami and huge amounts of ash being released that contributed to the demise of this great civilization with some theorists even suggesting that this event is what eventually provided the basis for Plato's Atlantis.

From the Archaic to the Classical Periods

During the Archaic period (800 – 500 BCE) kings gradually found themselves replaced by republics. Athens introduced democracy through single city-states instead of larger administrative regions, and the first Greek coins were minted; furthermore, this period also saw the first examples of the iconic pottery and sculpture ancient Greece is known for. It established a foundation for the new Classical period (480 – 323 BCE), also known as the golden age of Athens, it was a time when Pericles ordered the construction of the grand Acropolis, a building that still looks down upon Athens today. He also gave his renowned speech where he honored the men who fell while defending the city against the Persians at the Battle of Marathon and, but to name a few, the country saw great leaps in the arts, philosophy, the sciences and education. Many famous individuals such as Plato and Aristophanes also left their mark during this era. In 480 BCE another example of stories still told, King Leonidas and his legendary 300 Spartans were defeated at Thermopylae. Themistocles was victorious over the Persian navy at Salamis, which saw the Persians completely defeated at Plataea the following year.

Thus, the first democratic state was born: Athens. Democracy comes from the Greek words *Demos*, which means people, and *Kratos*, which means power. In this new democratic system – all be it limited – men over 20 were allowed to vote for government. Philosophers, including the likes of Thales, appeared during this time and began to voice their ideas regarding the natural world. Specifically, the philosophers Pythagoras, Xenophanes and Anaximander were able to reconsider pre-conceived ideas about the cosmos and present new theories about how the world came to be.

Those who followed, including Archimedes, carried on with these investigations, eventually allowing for the founding of formal mathematics. Socrates, Plato, and Aristotle developed their works to such an extent that they had a near immeasurable impact on Greece and the rest of the world. Architecture and artistic styles continued to progress, continuously moving away from the idyllic and turning towards realism. For example, the Parthenon marbles derive from this period, and although they feature mythical beings, they are shown in a much more realistic light when compared to earlier works.

In 480 BCE the Greeks finally overthrew the Persians and facilitated the development of artistic styles in combination with the growth of a stable economy. This caused Athens to quickly rise and become the dominant power in the ancient world, it also established a mighty navy and demanded tributes from various city-states around the Greek world. Athens also created the Delian League and named it after the island of Delos, this league consisted of a coalition of allies ready to defend each other from the Persians should they attempt to invade once more.

Sparta was a formidable military state to the south in Laconia and quickly established its own league because it did not trust Athens. Thus, the Peloponnesian League was named after the region where Sparta was located and known for its own politics, it also viewed Athens as a dictatorial state, one that could become a serious threat to both Sparta's economy and its people. When the tensions between Athens and Sparta finally became unbearable, a series of wars known as the Peloponnesian Wars ensued. The first war (460 – 445 BCE) concluded with a truce, whereas the second (431 – 404 BCE) resulted in Athens being destroyed by Sparta; however, Sparta celebrated only a bitter victory, because it was left severely depleted and weakened.

This period is generally referred to as the Late Classical Period. With Sparta and Athens no longer wielding any true power, the ensuing void was soon filled by a rising power from the north. Philip II of Macedon defeated Athens at the Battle of Chaeronea in 338 BCE and brought all of the Greek city-states under his control. Two years later he was assassinated leaving his son Alexander to lead the Greeks first back to regional, then world dominance.

Alexander the Great and the Rise of Rome

Alexander the Great is known as one of the world's all time preeminent military leaders. Born in 356 BCE he was inspired by his father's dream of overthrowing Persia in revenge for attempting to invade Greece decades earlier. When Alexander took his father's throne he assembled a mighty army consisting of nearly all the able men available to him. Well funded his campaign took him to Egypt, which then saw him sweep through Asia Minor into Persia, where – after securing his position as the king of the Persian Empire – he struck into the Indian subcontinent, seemingly intent on conquering the known world in its entirety. Alexander had studied under the great philosopher Aristotle, who had in turn been taught by Plato, thus as a result of Alexander's campaigns Greek philosophy and language quickly spread throughout the entire known world, which, at that time, the Greeks thought ended in India.

In 323 BCE Alexander the Great died and left the territory he once held to be divided among four of his greatest generals. This period is known as the Hellenistic era (323 – 31 BCE) during which Greek beliefs and ideas reached their peak. The generals were known as the Diodachi and for a time numerous power struggles took place between them, one of them, Antigonus, founded the Antigonid Dynasty in Greece but quickly fell from power before being restored by his grandson Antigonus II Gonatus.

It was also at this time that Rome began taking an interest in the Greek world; so much so that in 168 BCE the Roman Empire's forces met the Greek army at Pydna and gained a major victory that would change the course of history. Greece came to be influenced by Rome in many ways and in 146 BCE became a Protectorate, in turn the Romans borrowed heavily from Greek culture and society by adopting their religion, mythology, language and philosophy. After Octavian defeated Queen Cleopatra of Egypt and Mark Anthony at the Battle of Actium in 31 BCE, Octavian renamed himself Emperor Augustus and Greece was incorporated fully into the Roman Empire.

Ancient Egypt

Located in Africa, ancient Egypt has long fascinated and intrigued the world and as one of the earliest known civilizations it boasts a rich history and mesmerizing culture, which continues to inspire and intrigue historians and artists today.

Egypt's name is actually derived from the Greeks who knew it as *Aegyptos*, which was how the Greeks came to pronounce the Egyptians name for their Kingdom Hwt-Ka-Ptah, meaning the House of the Spirit of Ptah. So thus can a connection be made between the naming of Egypt and Ptah, one of the earliest deities to be worshipped in the region. During the Old Kingdom period the country was named Kemet, which translates as the 'Black Land'. This term refers to the plentiful black soil found on the banks of the River Nile that was home to the earliest settlements, eventually the Egyptians came to call their land Misr (meaning *country*) a term that is still used today.

Between 8,000 and 525 BCE Egypt was free of dominant outside influences and was renowned for its iconic architecture, artwork and sciences. Various monuments and structures still survive from this period, including many that modern day tourists visit Egypt to see for themselves.

Archaeologists, exploring the Sahara Desert, have unearthed evidence that suggests that around the 9th and 8th centuries BCE cattle were raised there, this, along with other artifacts, points to a flourishing civilization that grew through the establishment of agriculture. Since the soils were arid at this point, the hunter-gatherers settled near the life-giving waters of the River Nile sometime before 6,000 BCE. Systemized farming began around a thousand years later with the Badarian Culture emerging in around 5,500 BCE. Other cultures that followed the Badarian include the Amratian

(Nagada I), the Gerzean (Nagada II) and the Nagada Cultures (Nagada III).

Each of these cultures laid down the foundations for future Egyptian civilization and a written record of history began to be documented sometime between 3,400 and 3,200 BCE with the use of the Hieroglyphics Scripts that were established by the Nagada III culture. Mummification started at Hierakonpolis, with imposing stone tombs being erected at Abydos; the Palermo Stone is dated to around 3,000 BCE and indicates that Xois was already an ancient city and as time passed, the smaller settlements eventually developed into larger urban areas.

The Earliest History of Egypt

Dated to around 3,150 – 2,613 BCE the Early Dynastic period saw both Upper and Lower Egypt come together as one under the rule of King Menes. He ruled Upper Egypt and controlled the north from either 3,118 BCE or c. 3,150 BCE. This information is taken from the History of Egypt, a work by Manetho, a 3rd century BCE historian who lived during the Ptolemy Dynasty. There is some dispute amongst scholars on Manetho's chronology but his work still remains the most reliable source of early Egyptian events.

Indeed, Manetho is the sole source that tells of Menes conquering the north and uniting the two kingdoms. It is mostly agreed upon by scholars that Manetho's Menes was referring to King Narmer, a man who was able to unite the divided lands of Egypt under his rule, however, it should be noted that not all scholars identify Menes as King Narmer. Menes is sometimes associated with King Hor Aha, or Aha, who was supposedly his successor. Menes is also thought by some to be a title that translates to *he who endures* instead of the name of an actual person. Narmer ruled Lower Egypt from Hierakonpolis – and later Memphis –because the region is located in the north, which faces the Mediterranean Sea. Upper Egypt is actually located in the south. It is astonishing that the earliest rulers of this then unified kingdom constructed the iconic mastaba tombs (precursors to the pyramids) and developed their own unique burial rituals.

The Old Kingdom Period (c. 2,613 – 2,181 BCE) saw further developments in architecture because it was during this period that numerous timeless structures were built, including the pyramids and the Great Sphinx of Giza. Reigning around 2,670 BCE, King Djoser ordered the construction of the Step Pyramid after discussions with his ministers. The Step Pyramid was finished at Saqqara around 2,630 BCE and was designed by Imhotep – a great physician who wrote detailed notes of the remedies and treatments for over one hundred diseases and illnesses. Little did he know that one day in the future he too would go on to be deified and worshipped throughout the region, a god amongst the gods.

King Khufu commissioned the construction of the Great Pyramid of Giza – often referred to as the Pyramid of Cheops – the only surviving structure of the Seven Wonders of the Ancient World. Around 2,530 and 2,510 BCE, kings Khafre and Menkaure both built their own pyramids, all of which were encased in dazzling white limestone. Not only did they provide the eternal resting places for the kings, they showcased the wealth and prestige of the living gods on earth, because this is how ancient Egyptians perceived their rulers, as living deities. Over the years scholars have put forth various theories as to how these awe-inspiring monuments were constructed, especially considering the technology available at the time. Some scholars suggest that the technology used to construct the pyramids was far more advanced than what we know of and has subsequently been lost over time. Initially it was thought that these imposing structures were built using slaves, but current archaeological findings have debunked this story as it is now known that skilled architects, artists and workers received a salary for building these incredible monuments.

The First Intermediate Period

The initial key event that occurred during the First Intermediate Period (2,181 – 2,040 BCE) was the complete disintegration of the ruling class, an event that led to the kingdom being divided into several separate entities that became independent of each other. This resulted in two key centers emerging: Heirokonpolis and Thebes. New dynasties were established at both locations such that they then ruled a divided Upper and Lower Egypt. These dynasties continued to war with each other until 2,055 BCE, where upon Mentuhotep II finally reunited Egypt under Theban rule.

Under the Theban king Egypt entered the Middle Kingdom Period (2,040 – 1,782 BCE) that is also referred to the Classical Era, a time when, as Thebes grew prosperous, the economy stabilized and the arts flourished. The Egyptian kings pushed down into Nubia, establishing rule over the southern lands, and constructed forts to protect their trading posts. It was during this period that the River Nile flooded to such an extent that many suffered famine. With a sudden decline in Thebes' power Hyksos was able to gain influence over the entirety of Egypt.

Not much is known about the enigmatic Hyksos people but it is believed they originated from what is now modern day Syria around 1,800 BCE. The names of these foreign rulers are

Semitic in origin but scholars are still unable to determine what ethnic group they belonged to. The Hyksos people gained power gradually, eventually seizing Lower Egypt in 1720 BCE, with Upper Egypt ultimately becoming their vassal, the king a mere puppet instead of an actual ruler. This point in time is referred to as the Second Intermediate Period (1,782 – 1,570 BCE) because the Hyksos rulers now had control over the region and regardless of the hatred directed towards them the Hyksos introduced new revolutionary technology and weapons, such as the horse drawn chariot and the composite bow.

By 1,700 BCE the domain of Kush had become powerful in its own right and had allied itself with Hyksos against the Theban kingdom. The native Egyptians initiated numerous military campaigns to force the Hyksos from their lands and to overthrow Nubia, but all proved unsuccessful, this succession of failure continued until the arrival of Ahmose I from Thebes, who showed brilliant military strategy in reclaiming Egypt back from its foreign rulers.

The New Kingdom and the Religious Reforms

The rise of Ahmose I initiated what is now referred to as the New Kingdom Period (1,570 – 1,069 BCE). Egypt, reunited once more, experienced a period of social and economic stability, this period also saw the introduction of the title pharaoh, because prior to Ahmose I rulers were referred to as kings. Several of the iconic temples and structures around Thebes date from this time including Abu Simbel, the Karnak Temple, the Luxor Temple and the Valley of the Kings and Queens. Tuthmosis I made great leaps in expanding his influence and was able to push Egypt's borders through to the Euphrates River, Syria and Nubia. Furthermore, Queen Hatshepsut became the first female pharaoh when she succeeded him, successfully increasing the kingdom's trading networks to various other lands, including that of Punt. Queen Hatshepsut ruled for 22 peaceful years allowing Egypt to become very wealthy under her guidance. After her, Tuthmosis II tried in vain to have her legacy wiped clean from Egyptian history but was thankfully unsuccessful as her reign was one of peace, economic growth and expansion.

Although Tuthmosis III continued Queen Hatshepsut's policies, scholars believe he was not an advocate of women's rule or of seeing women take positions of supreme power, because he believed that only men had the right to do either. Many of her cartouches were destroyed in order to remove any influence she'd had on Egypt, both past and future, but when Tuthmosis died in 1,425 BCE he left a kingdom that had increased in power and prestige. For one, various types of beer were now available, which allowed the upper class a life of pleasure and ease, healthcare practices had improved and beautiful baths were established for leisure and enjoyment. Women's healthcare and contraception practices were recorded within the Kahun Gynecological Papyrus, which was written around 1,800 BCE and was used by Egyptian physicians. The Egyptians had access to surgeons and dentists who were gifted with some of the greatest skills to be found in the ancient world.

Amenhotep IV took the throne in 1,353 BCE and it wasn't long before he renamed himself Akhenaten, which translates to *the living spirit of Aten*, a change reflected in his singular devotion to the god Aten. Previously Egypt had worshipped a pantheon of deities, with Osiris, Ptah, Isis, Amunand and Hathor being the most popular amongst them. Akhenaten's popularity developed to such an extent that the priests became incredibly wealthy and held almost as much power as the pharaoh himself. Akhenaten and his wife Nefertiti turned their backs on the established religion and gods of the time and introduced the worship of Aten, it is because of this that historians believe it was they who introduced the world's first known monotheistic religion. The religious reforms Akhenaten introduced to the kingdom meant that the priests no longer held any real power, with the pharaoh once more going against the old traditions when he transferred the capital to a new site based at Amarna. This era is referred to as the Amarna Period and dates between 1,353 and 1,336 BCE, a time when the worship of the old gods was abolished.

However, these new religious beliefs and practices did not cement themselves amongst the Egyptian people and remained unpopular, with the only thing Akhenaten becoming famous for was his beautiful temple, in which he constructed a statue dedicated to his wife Nefertiti. As his rule progressed he was not able to meet the demands of the people, because, as historians believe, he focused his attention more on religious beliefs than that of his subjects' well being.

On Akhenaten's death his son was named pharaoh, originally given the title Tutankhaten the new leader, upon his coronation, came to be known as Tutankhamun. A name that even today readily identifies as being arguably one of the most recognizable pharaohs of ancient Egypt. He ruled between 1,336 to 1,327 BCE, where he reintroduced the religious practices connected to the worship of the old gods. He restored the old temples and attempted to remove all mention of the focus of his father's monolithic worship. The capital was also moved back to Thebes before he died unexpectedly at the age of 18 or 19, an event that delivered him to us as the pharaoh of the famous tomb discovered by Howard Carter in the 1920s. His death has sparked numerous theories as to whether he died from natural causes or whether he was murdered by his successor.

Ramesses II, also referred to as Ramesses the Great – and considered to be the greatest pharaoh to have lived during the New Kingdom Period – fathered over 100 children and created some of the most extravagant buildings Egypt, if not the world, had ever known. He led the Egyptians into battle against Muwatalli II of the Hittite Empire at Kadesh, and – although technically a stalemate – Ramesses II had himself depicted as a great Egyptian hero on public displays, even going as far as to commission a beautiful representation of the battle in which he led the Egyptians to victory on the walls of the temple at Abu Simbel.

As with Akhenaten before him he dedicated a temple to his own beautiful queen, and the first of The Great Royal Wives of Ramesses the Great, Nefertari, a name that actually means 'beautiful companion'. In 1,258 BCE he signed the Treaty of Kadesh, broadly recognised as the first peace treaty in history. He ruled until his death in 1,213 BCE and came to be the longest ruling pharaoh in Egyptian history.

The Deterioration of Egypt and the Arrival of Alexander the Great

Ramesses II's – having died – was succeeded by Rameses III, who continued to pursue his predecessor's policies. However, this incredibly wealthy kingdom had caught the attention of various neighbors, including the mysterious Sea Peoples, who had begun to raid the coastal towns of Egypt in hopes of becoming rich themselves. The origins of the Sea Peoples are unknown – just as with the Hyksos – but they are thought to have originated somewhere in the South Aegean, but from wherever they came, they caused mayhem between 1,276 and

1,178 BCE on the Egyptian coastline through savage and relentless attacks. This caused Ramesses III to become incensed to the point that he raised an army and defeated them in a great battle at Xois in 1,178 BCE.

However, political strife had crept inside the government and his successors had to deal with serious internal problems, for one, peoples living in conquered regions began to rebel against the pharaoh. After the reestablishment of the old gods the priests of Amun had amassed so much land and wealth that they had the power to destabilize the entire government, and court officials had become so corrupt that during the reign of Ramesses XI (1,107 – 1,077 BCE), the government could not function anymore, so much so that it completely collapsed leading to the Third Intermediate Period.

The Kushite King Piye was able to reunite the divided kingdom under his rule, allowing his domains to flourish once more. However in 671 BCE, Esarhaddon of Assyria began seriously testing the once secure borders and by 667 BCE he had taken control of the region through total warfare and left all in ruin.

On attacking Pelusium in 525 BCE, Cambyses II of Persia found that the Egyptians had long worshipped cats – because they were seen as representative of the cat-headed goddess Bast – and so it was that, along with other sacred Egyptian imagery, and before battle, Cambyses II had his men paint cats onto their shields. This helped the Persians in their fight against the deeply superstitious Egyptians who were forced to surrender; leaving Egypt in Persian hands until Alexander the Great arrived in 332 BCE.

Despite being a foreigner the Egyptians regarded Alexander of Macedon as their savior, namely because he took control of the country without any significant bloodshed, and then, on founding the city of Alexandria, he continued with his quest of conquering Asia Minor.

In 323 BCE Alexander the Great died, leaving his extensive empire to be divided between his four generals, with Ptolemy being the one who transported Alexander's body back to Alexandria. Here he established the last Egyptian dynasty, which is also known as the Ptolemaic Dynasty. Queen Cleopatra VII was the last of his dynasty and is famous for marrying Julius Caesar and then Mark Anthony of Rome. After her death Egypt became part of the Roman Empire until the fall of the Byzantine Empire where upon it fell to the Muslim Rashidun army.

The Roman Empire

Out of all the civilizations to emerge in the Western world the Roman Empire, which emerged from the post-Roman Republic period of the ancient Roman civilization, is often said to be the one that was – in terms of its political and social reach – the most widespread. When it was at its peak – around 117 CE – it had spread across much of modern day Europe, North Africa and parts of the Middle East. The amazing feats of the Roman Empire have most definitely left their mark on history, even today its legacy influences the legal system of many countries, including the United States, Canada, and the UK, and many aspects of education, language, religion and culture.

The Early Dynasties

After Augustus (Octavian) defeated the forces of Queen Cleopatra VII of Egypt and her husband Mark Anthony at the

Battle of Actium in 31 BCE, he declared himself the first Roman Emperor and became known as Augustus Caesar. His uncle was Julius Caesar, the former husband of Cleopatra, a man who is often stated to be the first emperor, but Julius Caesar never took the title and instead chose to take the role of a dictator. After Julius Caesar the Senate granted Octavian the title of emperor as a reward for annihilating powerful enemies and bringing stability back to Rome.

Augustus ruled the Roman Empire between 31 BCE and 14 CE where he established a series of religious and social reforms that continued to influence the empire and his heirs long after his death. Under his rule new laws were created, the borders were secured and various new buildings were constructed, cementing the reputation of Rome as one of the greatest powers in the ancient world. For two centuries Rome enjoyed the Pax Romana, which is also known as the Roman Peace. Augustus is therefore credited with creating a time of great harmony and prosperity in Rome.

Dying in 14 CE Augustus was succeeded by Tiberius, a man who carried on with many of the previous emperor's policies, but he lacked Augustus' personality and vision for Rome's future. Augustus, Tiberius, Caligula, Claudius and Nero were all part of the Julio-Claudian Dynasty. Caligula has long been known for his immorality and lunacy but his early reign was quite successful. It was the same for Claudius, who was able to expand Roman rule into Britannia (modern day Britain). This was something that even the great Julius Caesar had been unable to achieve, Nero though had issues from the very start and ended up committing suicide. Caligula ended up being killed by his guards and Claudius by his wife, after such a tumultuous period Rome eventually stumbled into the "Year of the Four Emperors" after the demise of Julio-Claudian rule.

On the event of Nero's death in 68 CE four men, Galba, Otho, Vitellius and Vespasian all took the throne in the space of one year. When Galba assumed power, it was clear that he wasn't fit to rule and the Praetorian Guard assassinated him at the first opportunity. The next individual to assume power was Otho who was believed to have been a good ruler by his contemporaries; however, Vitellius sought to seize power and initiated a short civil war that resulted in the death of Otho by his own hand. Thus, Vitellius effectively became the next emperor, but he fared no better than Galba, ignoring his responsibilities by spending extravagantly on feasts and entertainment. General Vespasian, encouraged by the Roman legions to march on Rome and assume power for himself, was declared Emperor of Rome precisely one year after Galba had taken the same title.

The period that followed the Year of the Four Emperors is known as the Flavian Dynasty. This era is recognized for its wealth, massive building projects and expansion of the empire's borders. Vespasian ruled for ten years and commissioned the construction of the world renowned Coliseum. It took a very long time to complete and was only finished during the reign of his son, Emperor Titus (79 – 81 CE), with further modifications made under the reign of Domitian (81 – 96 CE).

During Titus' reign Mount Vesuvius erupted and covered Pompeii/Herculaneum under a thick blanket of ash for almost two thousand years. Titus is given considerable credit for dealing with the aftermath of this eruption and the Great Fire of Rome that occurred the following year in 80 CE. His brother Domitian succeeded Titus in 81 CE when he died from a fever. Domitian was another successful ruler who helped

Rome recover from fire damage and stabilize the economy. While he was largely a good emperor, his tyrannical policies caused friction between himself and the Senate and because he continually disagreed with the Senate he was eventually assassinated in 96 CE.

The Five Good Emperors

On Domitian's assassination he was succeeded by Nerva; a man who had been his most trusted advisor. With Nerva came the founding of the Nervan-Antonin Dynasty that lasted between 96 and 192 CE and it was during this era that Rome saw a great expansion of its borders and an increase in wealth. This progress is often attributed to its rulers during this time, referred to as the Five Good Emperors. These five emperors were Nerva (96 – 98 CE), Trajan (98 – 117 CE), Hadrian (117 – 138), Antoninus Pius (138 – 161) and Marcus Aurelius (161 – 180 CE). It was due to the rule of these five emperors that the Roman Empire reached the heights of its power, with the military having strengthened to a level the likes of which had never been seen before. After Marcus Aurelius died, the last emperors of the Nervan-Antonin Dynasty were Lucius Verus and Commodus. Lucius Verus jointly ruled with Marcus Aurelius until the emperor died, and has long been regarded as somewhat of a buffoon because of his numerous foolish decisions. Commodus was the son of Marcus Aurelius and history portrays him to be one of the worst Roman emperors to have ever lived. In 192 CE, Commodus was strangled to death, his assassination perhaps masterminded by Pertinax, who rose to take power for himself.

The Severan Dynasty

Pertinax was only in power for three short months before he himself was killed. Eventually, Septimus Severus took control of the seat of power and reigned as Emperor between 193 and

211 CE. His reign begins what is referred to as the Severan Dynasty.

Septimus Severus ultimately conquered the Parthians and enlarged Rome's territory, unfortunately his military expeditions in Britannia and North Africa drained Rome's coffers and the empire began to experience financial problems. His sons Caracalla and Geta became joint-rulers upon his death, but it wasn't long before Geta found himself being murdered at the hands of his brother.

Caracalla reigned until 217 CE whereupon he too succumbed to a violent death, killed by his personal guard. During Caracalla's rule, free men – regardless of origin or past status – were allowed Roman citizenship, while sounding like a progressive gesture, it was most likely simply an ingenious way to collect ever more taxes to fill Rome's forever-dwindling finances. The dynasty carried on under the management of 'Empress' Julia Maesa until Alexander Severus was killed in 235 CE.

The Division of the Empire

During the 3rd century, a period referred to as the Imperial Crisis, Rome had to endure a civil war as numerous generals wrestled to take control. People experienced one hardship after another because the economy was failing and the empire eventually ended up being divided into three different areas. Diocletian brought these areas back together under his rule, which ran from 284 to 305 CE. He introduced the Tetrarchy – or the Rule of Four – to ensure order could be effectively maintained. However, Diocletian discovered that the empire had expanded to such an extent that it was difficult to rule; therefore in 285 CE he divided it into the Eastern Roman Empire, based in Byzantium, and the Western Roman Empire, based in Rome, which allowed the whole – as two – to be effectively governed. Since much of the Imperial Crisis was caused by fighting over who the next successor would be he declared that a successor was required to be named as soon as an emperor took power. In 305 CE Diocletian volunteered to step down, and when he died in 311 CE his general Maxentius and successor Constantine threw the empire back into a bloody civil war.

Constantine and Christianity

The Battle of the Milvian Bridge – over the River Tiber, Rome – in 312 CE saw Constantine overpower Maxentius, an event that allowed him to become the sole ruler of the two halves of the Roman Empire. He reigned between 306 and 337 CE and credited his victory to Jesus Christ, a belief that saw him establish the Edict of Milan in 317 CE, an act that gave people the freedom of religious belief. This behavior on his part saw an increased tolerance towards the "new religion", a belief system that would later come to be known as Christianity. Previously, earlier Roman rulers had forged ties with a particular god or goddess to boost their authority and prestige; for example, Julius Caesar claimed he was descended from the goddess Venus on his father's side, however, Constantine – instead of choosing one of the Roman deities – decided to follow in Jesus Christ to cement his divine rights.

At the First Council of Nicaea, in 325 CE, Constantine oversaw the council to both organize the new religion and to decide on critical theological issues such as the divinity of Christ. Texts were selected so as to decide whether they should be included in the official religious canon known as the Bible. Under Constantine's leadership The Roman Empire once more stabilized and the economy grew. A new city known as New Rome was built where modern day Istanbul now resides, but was later renamed Constantinople. Christian writers refer to him as Constantine the Great because he was so devoted towards his faith. Upon his death he was succeeded by his sons who quickly led the empire into a series of bloody wars, undoing all of the hard work their father had achieved during his rule.

Constantine II, Constantius II and Constans were the given names of his three sons, and they separated the territory amongst themselves. After a few battles, Constantine II and Constans died, which left Constantius II as emperor. He named his cousin Julian to succeed him. On taking the throne Julian only reigned for two years – 361 to 363 CE. He attempted to bring back some of Rome's past glories through a series of reorganization in the government, he forced Christian officials from their posts, banned their faith, banned preaching of the scriptures and excluded all Christians from joining the army. Julian was the last pagan emperor of the Roman Empire and is set to be perpetually known as Julian the Apostate.

The next emperor was Jovian, a man who reintroduced Christianity and who annulled all of Julian's religious reforms, but it was Theodosius I who took on the responsibility of leading the empire. Ruling between 379 and 395 CE he banned all pagan worship, transformed pagan temples into Christian churches and shut down educational centers. Indeed, it was Theodosius I who shut down Plato's Academy in Greece. While many Romans were Christian, the majority was still faithful to paganism, so, because of this, the Roman aristocracies were not in favor of his reforms. Theodosius I devoted his time to the reestablishment of Christianity throughout the Roman Empire, so much so that he ignored many of his responsibilities. He also came to be the very last emperor that ruled both halves of the empire.

The Fall of the Roman Empire

Between 376 and 382 CE Rome underwent a series of wars against the Goths known as the Gothic Wars. Emperor Valens lost at the Battle of Adrianople, which triggered the beginning of the Roman Empire's decline.

Scholars cannot agree on the exact reason why the empire fell because there are likely a plethora of reasons, but the historian Edward Gibbon suggests that it was Christianity that caused the fall of this mighty empire, because it lacked the sensibilities to support the social customs of the Roman people as they had once existed. Others suggest that the empire's administrative structure was simply stretched too thin to protect itself from outsiders and foreign invasions. Yet another theory is that it couldn't support its citizens due to economic problems, the amount of food available was scarce and the government was not able to effectively collect taxes. It was because of these internal reasons, and vicious external raids from the Visigoths, that Rome began to deteriorate rapidly.

The Western Roman Empire fell on September 4, 476 CE when King Odoacer overthrew Emperor Romulus Augustus; however, it is important to note that various other scholars mark the end of the Empire as 480 CE when Julius Nepos died. The Eastern Roman Empire carried on as the Byzantine Empire, lasting until 1453, yet, regardless the exact date of its demise, the Roman Empire's legacy influenced many newer civilizations and is one of the greatest empires to have ever existed.

Chapter 2– Asian History

Over several thousand years Asia has witnessed the rise and fall of some incredible civilizations. These include, to name but a few, those of the Chinese Empire (one of the longest reigning cultures in world history), of India and the Khmer's – centered in what is now present day Cambodia.

India

The South Asian country of India takes its name from the mighty Indus River but the land itself is often referred to as Bharata, a reference to a legendary emperor whose tale is retold to some extent within the Mahabharata. The 5th century CE texts, called the Puranas, tell us how Bharata managed to seize control over India and ruled peacefully for many years, giving the reason as to why India was once called Bharatavarsha. The archaeological record shows that the earliest known humans to have lived there did so from some 250,000 years ago, making it one of the oldest continually occupied areas of the planet.

Archaeological findings have unearthed a variety of artifacts that were used by those who lived there, including various kinds of stone tools. Ancient India is often overlooked – while other ancient civilizations such as Egypt, Rome and Greece are praised for contributing to various disciplines, concepts and academic areas – which, when you come to think about it, is rather odd, because it was India that gave us the number zero and the place value-system.

Pre-History of India

According to archaeologists modern-day India, Nepal and Pakistan have been inhabited by humans for over 250,000 years, including Homo heidelbergensis, a predecessor of contemporary Homo sapiens. Homo heidelbergensis had been present in the Indian sub-continent long before Homo sapiens established themselves across Europe. While archaeologists concentrated on excavations of these early humans within Europe and the Middle East, India was essentially overlooked until the early 20th century, and although scholars had been aware of the ancient culture of Harappa since the mid-19th century, they did not realize its significance. Instead they concentrated on finding the locations of areas mentioned in the Mahabharata and the Ramayana, written in or around the 5th or 4th centuries BCE. They discounted any chance of finding sites that predate these periods because they did not think they would find anything significant. Even on discovering sites of interest archaeologists did not begin to excavate and study them until the late 20th century, but then – after a lot of hard work – a key historical site was found at Balathal, which dates to around 4,000 BCE.

In the last five decades archaeologists have worked on these new sites and increased our understanding of early Indian history, for example at Balathal, archaeologists discovered a 4,000 year old skeleton in 2009. The individual is believed to have suffered from leprosy, which is the earliest example of the disease in the country. Before its discovery scholars believed the disease had established itself amongst the region's human population much later on in history. In fact it was originally believed to have originated in Africa, being brought to the sub-continent via the armies of Alexander the Great in 323 BCE. Furthermore, excavations have shown that humans became more active in India during the Holocene Era (around 10,000 years ago). This clearly demonstrates that our insights into the region need to be reconsidered, especially since most of our knowledge of ancient history – certainly in the West – comes from a focus on Egypt, Rome, Greece and the Middle East. It has long been assumed that the Vedic customs emerged after the Aryan migration to India around 1,500 BCE, but it now seems likely that they originated from the local populations that settled at places such as those found at the Balathal archaeological site located in Vallabhnagar tehsil of Udaipur district of Rajasthan state in western India.

Mohenjo-Daro and Harrapan Civilization

Dating from around 5,000 BCE the Indus Valley Civilization is one of the earliest civilizations to emerge from the Indian sub-continent, spreading through the lower Ganetic Valley area all the way up to Malwa. The urban centers that developed here were much larger compared to modern day towns in other countries and were strategically laid out according to cardinal points. Buildings were constructed out of mud bricks and mostly fashioned from kilns with dwellings built with a courtyard, a front door, a kitchen area and rooms for sleeping. Most family activities were carried out near the front of the home in the courtyard because it was a spacious area that could accommodate everyone in the family. The houses were similar to what is believed to have existed throughout the ancient Middle East, Rome and Greece.

The most significant sites from this period are Mohenjo-Daro and Harappa. Both these sites were originally in India before the 1947 partition – when India became two separate nations – the other being the country that we now know as Pakistan. The Harrapan Civilization is also known as the Indus Valley Civilization and takes its name from the site of Harappa. It is generally separated into the Early Period (5,000 – 4,000 BCE), Middle Period (4,000 – 2,900 BCE) and the Mature Period (2,900 – 1,900 BCE).

Harappa can be dated to the Middle Period and was established sometime around 3,000 BCE, the Mohenjo-Daro was founded during the Mature Period and built around 2,600 BCE. During the 19th century the British used large amounts of the materials found at Harappa to build a railway, the structures having already slowly suffered damage over time due to the villagers of Harappa using them to construct their own buildings. Archaeologists have had a difficult time excavating the area because of the destruction caused by both the local populous and the British. Little is known except that it was one of the most significant Bronze Age sites in India, if not the world, that had an estimated population of around 30,000 inhabitants.

However, all is not lost and there are things to be learned from Mohenjo-Daro. Until 1922 the ancient city lay buried under the earth, in fact – in the Sindhi language – the name can be translated as "Mound of the Dead". Unfortunately, we do not know what its original name was, although a number of theories have been put forward from the artifacts found in the area. One artifact mentions the name Kukkutarma, which translates to "City of the Cock", a name that suggests the city may have been famous for either the fighting or breeding of cocks.

Archaeological excavations show that the city was designed with streets laid at right angles with a complex drainage arrangement, and that close to the center of the site was a structure known as the Great Bath, which was heated and became one of the most famous buildings for those who lived there. Mohenjo-Daro was home to some exceptionally skillful workers who were able to work in and fashion tin, copper, lead and bronze. The evidence for this claim comes from the statue of the Dancing Girl, which is made from bronze and is sculpted in a very precise manner. They were able to grow and cultivate cotton, peas, wheat, barley and sesame, as the inhabitants of the city were mostly traders who brought goods from various other regions and kingdoms both near and far. There are also ancient texts from Mesopotamia that may refer to India or Mohenjo-Daro by the name Meluhha or Magan, furthermore, a number of artifacts that originated from the Indus Valley Civilization have been discovered at Mesopotamian sites.

We know from archaeological findings that the people living in Harappa worshipped a variety of deities and practiced their own rituals. There are statues of numerous deities including the storm god Indra, and terracotta statues of the Mother Goddess Shakti. Around 1,500 BCE, a new people, known as the Aryans, migrated into the country via the Khyber Pass and mixed with the existing population, who, in addition to bringing their own deities with them, are said to have introduced the use of horses. The newcomers were also nature worshippers or pantheists who worshipped the sun, so it is unlikely that their gods had human qualities, unlike the locals' deities who were anthropomorphic in nature.

It was also at this time (1,700 – 1,500 BCE) that Harappa seems to have suffered a decline in its culture. Although scholars have put forth various theories, it is generally accepted that it was due to climate change, about nine meters of silt at the Mohenjo-Daro site suggests that the Indus River experienced many floods, which caused the people to abandon the cities they'd established there. However, another popular theory that looks to support the reasons for Harrapan decline is the arrival of the Aryans with some scholars suggesting the Aryans invaded and pillaged the area, which in turn left many people displaced. Evidence for this theory comes from the vitrification of certain areas of Mohenjo-Daro, which exhibit signs of having come into contact with large amounts of heat. Whenever this phenomenon is observed at other sites across the world it is thought to be indicative of either war or battle, where the resulting fires have ravaged the environment. Conspiracy theorists have also suggested that the city was "destroyed by aliens" but these theories are not believable and are, on the whole, instantly discredited.

The Vedic Period

The arrival and subsequent influence of newcomers led to the beginning of what is regarded as the Vedic Period (1,700 – 150 BCE). This period is marked by a rustic lifestyle and dedication to the Vedas, which is a collection of religious scriptures. During this time, the people were separated into four social classes known as the Varnas or the caste system. Scholars and priests were known as the Brahmana and sat at the top of the caste system; warriors or Kshatriya came next, followed by the farmers and traders who were known as the Vaishya. The laborers were second from the bottom and were called the Shudra, lastly, there was another caste known as the Dalits or the untouchables, who were regarded as being at the bottom of the system. Their job was to mainly handle waste, and the products of dead animals such as meat and leather.

Initially the caste system was simply a reflection of the occupation one held, but over time it seems to have transformed into a hierarchy categorized by birth. People could not change what caste they were born into and could only change to a new caste through inter-marriage. This system became so entrenched because it came to be believed that an individual's status was determined not by you yourself, but by an all-powerful deity.

It is generally accepted that the religious beliefs of the Vedic Period date back to earlier times, however, these beliefs became formally established as the Sanatan Dharma or the Eternal Order, eventually becoming what we recognize today as the Hindu religion. The name Hinduism originated from the Indus River where people used to come to worship together, with the Sanatan Dharma referring to a set place for everything that exists. Humans, animals, plants and all other beings are meant to live in harmony with one another. This is partly why Hindus are generally vegetarians; they view the killing of animals as something that disrupts the Sanatan Dharma.

While Hinduism is known as a polytheistic faith, some Hindus see it as a monotheistic religion. This is because there is one deity Brahman – or The Self – whose different aspects are divided among the Hindu pantheon, the Hindus also believe that Brahman sets the eternal order and sustains the Universe while keeping a balance between everything. Throughout the Vedic era various traditions were formed as the Hindu religion progressed and the population increased. A number of religious texts emerged including the Ramayana, the Puranas, the Upanishads and the Mahabharata.

During the 6th century BCE India saw great religious change due to Vardhaman Mahavira (549 – 477 BCE) and Siddhartha Gautama (563 – 483 BCE). Both of these individuals denounced the traditional religious beliefs and founded their own religions, namely Jainism and Buddhism. As a result many city-states were built and soon expanded with growing populations due to the popularity of these religions. India's reputation grew as the country flourished, and as villages grew into major urban centers Cyrus of Persia turned his attention towards India. In 530 BCE he planned a military campaign and marched in, within ten years he had gained complete control. Darius I, a person who forced his own belief system and culture upon the Indian people, succeeded Cyrus, and although much of Persian culture still exists today, the Hindus were mostly able to preserve their identity and religious practices.

The Great Empires of Ancient India

Northern India remained under the control of the Persian Empire until the arrival of Alexander the Great in 327 BCE who, within a year, had conquered the Achaemenid Empire and taken over. Once more India was subjected to outside influences, which led to the emergence of a Greco-Buddhist philosophy. Buddha, originally known as Siddhartha Gautama, was depicted as wearing Greek clothes in new statues, but after Alexander the Great withdrew the country saw the rise of the Maurya Empire (322 – 185 BCE) with Chandragupta Maurya (322 – 298 BCE) as its leader. Northern India remained under its control until the latter part of the 3rd century BCE.

Bindusara was the son of Chandragupta who ruled from 298 to 272 BCE. He was able to expand the borders of the empire until he had control of the entire sub-continent, his son, Ashoka the Great (304 – 232 BCE) was a leader who ruled India between 269 and 232 BCE. During the eighth year of his reign Ashoka destroyed the city state of Kalinga, where over 100,000 people were massacred. Death and destruction caused him to convert to Buddhism and he began teaching peaceful principles to everyone he met. Throughout the rest of his life Ashoka donated great amounts of wealth to Buddhist temples and towns, however, his generous donations created a rift between himself and his officials. The government treasury was drained to such an extent that many officials began to withdraw their support, in fact it is specifically mentioned that his grandson, who held a position as a primary official in the empire, strongly opposed him. When Ashoka eventually died the treasury was empty and was a major reason as to why the empire began to collapse rapidly.

India came to be divided into countless smaller kingdoms and empires including the famous Kushan Empire. This part of Indian history is referred to as the Middle Period and is recognized for its increased trading with the Roman Empire, also referred to as the Indian Golden Age, the country saw the flourishing of arts throughout its numerous mini-kingdoms.

The Gupta Empire emerged around 240 BCE and was led by Sri Gupta or Lord Gupta between 240 and 280 CE. Lord Gupta is regarded as being part of the Vaishya caste, that is, he came from a group that was not part of the elite and is why historians consider his ascension to rule as being a peculiar phenomenon. Lord Gupta reorganized the government and assigned officials to maintain the rights of the people, as many injustices were occurring between the lower and upper classes. While the Guptas were in power, during what is known as the Indian Golden Era, society enjoyed a peaceful time. Architecture, philosophy, technology, astronomy and various other subjects were recorded in books but almost all of them have been lost over time.

During the Gupta Empire a number of important structures were built including the Puranas of Vyasa, the Ellora caves and Ajanta caves, the caves were richly decorated and built with very high ceilings. The Shakuntala and the Kamasutra were both created by Kalidasa, who borrowed from past works constructed by Vatsyayana. Arybhatta made several history changing mathematical discoveries including the number zero.

The Decline of Empire and the Arrival of Islam

The Gupta Empire came to be ruled by a series of weak leaders, which not surprisingly resulted in its steady decline. In 550 CE the Gupta Empire came to a screeching halt when Harshavardhana – a Buddhist Jat emperor – ruling between 590 and 647 CE, gained control. He was a well-educated man who had written three plays in addition to a number of other literary works and, known as a dedicated Buddhist, he encouraged the arts and opposed the slaughtering of animals – although he was not averse to killing men on the battlefield. Out of all the battles he fought in his lifetime, he only lost once. As a great military tactician his reign saw Northern India blossom – even if it was for a short period of time – once again. Both the Gupta Empire and Harshavardhana had stopped foreign invasions during their lifetime and brought relative peace amongst the different people's they ruled, but after their demise, the smaller kingdoms fell to squabbling amongst themselves once more.

In 712 CE Muhammed bin Quasim invaded India and took control over what is now modern day Pakistan. The Muslim armies established a new era and the old indigenous empires came to an end, and it was from this point onwards that India saw a rise in the number of independent city-states. Islamic monotheism, although only established in some parts of India, saw many convert to the new religion. The Muslims continued to rule parts of India until the mid-20th century whereupon Portugal, France and Britain came to colonize and control vast swathes of the Indian subcontinent.

Ancient Korea

Located in East Asia the Korean Peninsula is bounded by the Sea of Japan in the east, the Yellow Sea in the west and the Korea Strait in the south and has been occupied by humans since the Neolithic era. During the latter part of the first millennium BCE a new kingdom emerged by the name of Gojoseon and has come to be recognised as the first state in Korean history. Between the 1st century BCE and the 7th century CE this region was under the control of three kingdoms: Silla, Goguryeo and Baekje. With help from the Chinese, Silla was able to conquer the other kingdoms and take complete control of the peninsula whereupon it established the Unified Silla Kingdom. It continued to rule over the peninsula until it fell in 935 CE. The Goryeo kingdom was next to rule and did so until the Mongols swept through the region in the 13th century.

Despite periods of tension and warfare the kingdoms of Korea and China forged close relations with each other for mutual benefit, notably trade. Japan also traded with its neighbor and maintained diplomatic ties with Korea. Over the centuries ancient Korea contributed to many human achievements including portable metal printing and the stunning Silla gold crowns. It also came up with hanjie, which was one of the most well known types of paper and the ondol, a type of underground heating.

Gojoseon

According to the Samguk Yusa or Memorabilia of the Three Kingdoms – a 13th century text that is a collection of legends, folktales and historical accounts – Gochoson or Gojoseon (the first Korean nation) was established in 2,333 BCE. Dangun Wangeom was the founder and was believed to be the son of the deity Hwanung by his subjects. The fable continues and says that his mother was a she-bear who had taken the form of a woman. Nonetheless, archaeologists have determined that the civilization began as a coalition of several towns close to the Daedong and Liao River areas sometime between the 7th and 4th centuries BCE. Sima Qian, the famous ancient Chinese historian, mentions the state in his *Records of the Grand Historian*, which is dated to around 100 BCE. There is still some debate as to whether Gojoseon could actually be referred to as a state at this point in time. It is still unclear as to how much territory it controlled, where the capital was located and when it was established.

Gojoseon began to thrive as it made advancements in agriculture by utilizing various natural resources such as zinc, gold, copper, silver and tin. Various tools were imported from China and it was around this time that the ondol underground heating system was developed to allow for a better lifestyle in cold weather. The earliest Korean stoneware was grey in color and was also created around the same time. Gojoseon began to attract the attention of the Yan state around 300 BCE when it was afflicted by a series of successive attacks that were launched on the peninsula. Wiman Joseon of Korea tried to battle the Han Dynasty of China but failed miserably during the 2nd century BCE with the Han Dynasty effectively establishing its rule by enacting new laws in favor of China. The Chinese wanted the rich natural resources of Korea and so separated the country into four regions that were successfully governed by the Chinese.

The territory once held by Gojoseon changed its name to Goguryeo (also referred to as Koguryo). Meanwhile the southern part of the peninsula was separated into what is called the Three Hans of Chinhan, Mahan and Pyonhan. These Three Hans were also called Silla, Gaya and Baekje during the

Three Kingdoms era. Those who had been displaced from Gojoseon migrated south and took with them a complex culture and society.

Three Kingdoms Period

The Three Kingdoms Period occurred between 57 BCE and 668 CE and although there were only originally three kingdoms, a fourth "state" named Gaya had gained power by this time and was competing with Silla, Goguryeo and Baekje to gain dominance over the peninsula. In the Historical Records of the Three Kingdoms, also known as the Samguk sagi, it is stated that these clashes began during the 1st century BCE; however, although archaeologists generally agree they began during the 2nd or 3rd centuries CE some scholars suggest a later date, when the states began showing signs of having a more central government.

The capital of Goguryeo was located at Pyongyang – North Korea's modern day capital – and began to prosper during the 5th century CE under the rule of Gwanggaeto the Great (391 – 413 CE). Goguryeo expanded its borders and seized land north of the peninsula known as Manchuria, located in modern day Mongolia and northeast China.

At the same time Silla, ruled by King Beopheung (r. 514 – 540 CE), had its capital at Kumsong or modern day Gyeongjo. His government was much more organized and structured than Gwanggaeto's and he often emphasized the need for agriculture, even to the extent that he established a sophisticated irrigation system that included the use of primitive ploughs.

Gaya, on the other hand, did not develop into a structured kingdom. The famous Pon Kaya may well have been the

50

capital of Gaya but being located between two powerful states with powerful armies did not bode well, with Gaya eventually falling to Silla in 532 CE.

During the 4th century BCE, the state of Baekje prospered under the leadership of King Kunchogo. He founded his capital at Hansong or contemporary Gwangju and eventually formed an alliance with the kingdom of Silla, and from 433 to 553 CE Baekje and Silla enjoyed a relatively peaceful existence. However, in 554 CE, a battle between the two kingdoms broke out at the Kwansan-song Fortress in modern day Okchon when the Baekje state attempted to take back lands Silla had seized earlier. The Baekje army was brutally defeated and 30,000 soldiers were killed, it also marked the death of their ruler, King Song.

Over time the political structure and habits of government remained very similar, the king would rule with the help of senior officials chosen from the aristocratic class, while tribal leaders appointed by the central government administrated the provinces, who in turn collected taxes from the regions. Sometimes the central government would take payment in the form of men to help construct defensive structures. Slaves were very much part of early Korean culture and were usually those who had been captured during times of warfare, but criminals and people who were deeply in debt could also be made slaves. The slaves worked for the aristocracy, tended their lands and were paid meager wages if any at all. The people were divided into various social classes because the nobility felt the need to develop a barrier between themselves and the peasant classes. The class structure was ultimately based on Silla's bone rank system, where one's birth determined an individual's position in society; taxes were calculated based on either the type of work a person did or their birth status.

In any case, the Three Kingdoms and the Fourth State were forced to set aside their internal problems and concentrate on a new threat: the Chinese invasion from the north. The Chinese attempted to invade Goguryeo in the 7th century CE during the Sui and the Tang Dynasties and their strategy – to raid various points of the border simultaneously – was anticipated by Goguryeo, who was able to plan ambushes at weak points across the border. Ultimately the Chinese were unsuccessful in their invasion. In 644 CE the Chinese Tang Dynasty tried once more to invade but General Yang Manchun of Goguryeo was victorious in rebuffing the attack. Goguryeo now allied itself with Baekje after China formed a treaty with Silla to conquer Goguryeo and Baekje. Silla quickly raised an army of 50,000 men under the command of General Kim Yushin and waited for the command to begin the assault. Along with a naval force of 130,000 men, sent from China, Silla was eventually able to defeat Baekje and Uija, the king of Baekje, was taken to China against his will after the battle.

Pyongyang fared no better because it collapsed seven years later on suffering a crushing defeat. One year later King Pojang of Goguryeo and 200,000 of his people were also forcefully taken to China. Silla decided that it was never going to lower itself to act as a vassal state for the Chinese Empire and met the Chinese armies at Maesosong in 675 CE, the fight lasted for an entire year until Silla finally emerged as the victor on the plains of Kibolpo. In 668 CE Silla formed a government that now governed the whole of Korea and thus founded the Unified Silla Kingdom.

Unified Silla Kingdom

Historians generally believe that the Unified Silla Kingdom (668 - 935 CE) was the earliest dynasty to have dominion over the peninsula. In the northern part of the region there was a separate state known as Balhae or Parhae that distinguished itself from the rest of the kingdom, but the majority of its land was located in Manchuria, so many scholars do not acknowledge it as being part of what could be referred to as Korea proper.

The Unified Silla Kingdom was separated into nine provinces and five minor capital cities. Kumsong, or better known as Sorabol at the time, remained the main capital and experienced a major renovation project. Numerous buildings and structures were constructed including palaces, temples and pagodas. Nearly one million people lived in the city at its peak, a huge number at that time in history.

The central government reorganized the administrative system all the way down to the smallest village with the ruling families, their extended families and troublemakers forced to relocate elsewhere. Furthermore, the sons of village leaders were forced to send their first male children to work in the capital's administration buildings or within the army. There were significant advances in the agricultural sector due to sophisticated irrigation planning and a series of trading networks were mapped throughout East Asia, and it was because of this – and an absence of warfare – that the arts and sciences experienced considerable development during this time.

From the 8th century onwards the Unified Silla Kingdom experienced a slow decline mainly due its strict class structure, which was still determined by the bone rank system. Ideas were scarce and inspiration was low because there was a distinct lack of social movement and as time passed the elite became increasingly resentful of the king's power. The peasants already had a negative view of the upper class because they felt they were being exploited by heavy taxes. Furthermore, people from the landed aristocratic class were rioting to such an extent that the government could not keep them in line.

Finally it was two men who would cause the most anxiety for the Silla rulers. Gyeon Hwon or Kyon Hwon was a leader of the peasants and reestablished the old Baekje Kingdom in 892 CE; typically referred to as the Later Baekje. Around the same time a Buddhist monk, Gung Ye or Kungye, founded another Goguryeo Kingdom, the Later Goguryeo, to the north in 901 CE. These powers struggling for dominance finally plunged Korea back into civil war, closely mirroring the Three Kingdoms Period.

Historians call this era the Later Three Kingdoms period and in 927 CE, Kyon Hwon hit Kumsong with a brutal attack, meanwhile Gung Ye was assassinated by one of his own people because his followers had begun to hate his tyrannical methods. Wang Geon succeeded him in 918 CE and immediately attacked Later Baekje, which was suffering from internal strife. He then turned to Silla with hordes of cavalry and a vast array of archers, such were the forces under his command that the last king of Silla, Kyongsun, surrendered in 935 CE. Wang Geon emerged as the final victor and was able to reunite his country under the new Goryeo Dynasty.

Goryeo

The Goryeo Dynasty ruled the Korean peninsula between 918 and 1392 CE and it is from this word that the modern name for Korea in English is derived. Wang Geon established Songdo (modern day Kaesong) as his new dynasty's capital and declared himself king, such is his legacy that after his death his name was changed to King Taejo which means "Great Founder". Even in its early days the kingdom caught the attention of various other states that were looking to expand their territories, the Khitan attempted to invade the state twice, only to be completely defeated in 1033 CE, but in order to help secure its future Goryeo eventually constructed a fortified wall that extended across its northern borders.

Goryeo prospered and flourished to such a degree that Songdo alone had more than a thousand stores for food supplies. In 996 CE Goryeo began to mint its own coins and the first unbyong silver vases were produced in 1101 CE, they were even used as currency because they displayed the official seals set by the government.

Portable metal printing and the older woodblock form of printing were further developed during this time, while Buddhism became the major religion with numerous religious texts being authored by Koreans. Kim Pu-sik penned the very popular "History of the Three Kingdoms" in 1145 CE.

However, there was a darker side to the prosperity Goryeo experience and it wasn't long before corruption spread throughout the state. Rebellions occurred in 1126 and then again in 1135 and although the rebellions were quickly crushed, the people remained unhappy. It was during the reign of King Uijong that they began to openly criticize the funds being spent to construct extravagant palaces and water parks for the king's amusement. In 1170, the military overthrew the king and replaced him with his brother Myeongjong.

Myeongjong was essentially a puppet who was not able to govern his people well, the country soon became overrun by internal fighting that lasted for decades, thus it is that this period is primarily defined by various rebellions, assassinations and uprisings. Yet these tumultuous times were destined to appear relatively peaceful after the arrival of one Asia's most prolific warriors, Genghis Khan.

Up until the Great Khan, Mongolia had consisted of scattered tribes, but Ghengis Khan, bringing them all under his rule, was able to totally crush any resistance and was able to spread his army across most of Asia and to the doors of Europe.

Goryeo, however, had been miraculously left untouched, that is until the son of Ghengis Khan (Ogedei Khan) looked towards its borders in 1231 CE. Within a year Goryeo's capital had transferred to Kanghwa Island where the ruling classes were safe from the Mongolian hoard. However, raiders still managed to attack a total of six times during the following 30 years and in 1258 the military ruler was killed and the king was reinstated with every power he once possessed. Goryeo forged a peace treaty with Mongolia but did not gain its independence until General Yi Song-gye founded the Joseon Dynasty.

China

The Chinese Empire has long fascinated historians and artists because of its rich culture. It is one of the largest countries in the world and considered to be the oldest civilization in world history. China takes its name from the Sanskrit word *Cina*, which in turn is derived from the Qin Dynasty. Although the Qin Dynasty was the first imperial dynasty, it is referred to as the fourth dynasty after the Xia and Shang Dynasties. Both the

Greeks and the Romans called this empire "Seres", which translates to "Where the Silk comes from", because silk was transported frequently along the Silk Road from China to the West. The first recorded instance of the name "China" can be found within the journals of Barbosa that were written in 1516. Marco Polo – the renowned Venetian explorer – called the country "Cathay", whereas the Chinese referred to their own country Zhongguo, which means "The Middle Kingdom".

The history of China is divided into 19 legitimate dynasties with more than 100 so-called illegitimate dynasties. The Xia Dynasty is considered to have existed during the first period, which dates between 2,070 and 1,600 BCE. For a long time it was thought that the Xia Dynasty was a mere myth, but recent excavations have revealed sites that provide proof of its existence. Artifacts, bronze works, and burial sites show there was definitely a native civilization that existed during this time.

According to legend it was Yu the Great who established the Xia Dynasty (2070 BC). Yu is believed to have been a nobleman who worked for thirteen years to subdue the flow of the Yellow River, a river that always posed a serious problem because it constantly flooded, destroying people's crops. Chinese legend states that Yu would labor day and night to build dams for the people, so they began to praise him openly and eventually followed him. Shun was the ruler at the time who named Yu as his heir and continued to rule until he died. When Yu came to power he founded a new systematic approach to appointing heirs, an idea that led to the formation of what is known today as dynasties. The rulers and the elite classes lived in major urbanized centers while the peasants lived in the countryside.

On Yu's death Qi, his son, took the throne and continued the Xia Dynasty. This series of appointed rulers continued until Jie of the Xia Dynasty (1600 BC) came to power, a ruler who oppressed the people in almost every way imaginable and to such an extent that it is generally accepted that he was extremely ruthless and only cared for his own pleasures. When Tang of the Shang kingdom heard about this he gathered his men and attacked Jie.

Jie's army was eventually defeated after a long and brutal battle known as the Battle of Mingtiao. The people had mixed feelings about this, because although they no longer had to bow down to an oppressive ruler, there was now a new ruler from a different tribe who was foreign to many of them. In any case, Tang promised the people he would be a just ruler and thus founded the Shang Dynasty.

The Shang Dynasty lasted between 1,600 – 1,046 BCE. Tang originated from the Shang kingdom and is generally accepted to have lived between 1,675 and 1,646 BCE. However, the events that occurred during this time do not match with the events ascribed to him, but what we do know is that Tang was either the king or at he very least an extremely significant figure from the Shang kingdom. During his reign he lowered taxes, abolished the expensive construction projects that were initiated by Jie and generally ruled wisely. The country made great strides in the arts by creating various sculptures and literary works, with the earliest writing system having being established during the Shang Dynasty.

Before the Shang Dynasty the Chinese people used to worship a variety of deities including the highest god Shangti. This structure was similar to that of the ancient Greeks, where Zeus was at the head of the pantheon. Shangti was believed to be the Great Ancestor of the people and the patron god of agriculture, so believers looked towards Shangti to guide them through strife and hard times. Nonetheless, since Shangti was so far removed from the people, they required something more accessible, and it was this dilemma that eventually led to ancestor worship, with the Chinese beginning to believe that a deceased person was granted divine abilities.

This caused many of the living to call upon their ancestors in times of need, an idea which was further developed into a series of complex religious ceremonies that were conducted to appease the spirits of the dead. Decorated tombs were built to hold both the deceased and the belongings and items supposedly needed in the afterlife. Furthermore, the king was thought to have the ability to act as an intermediary between his living subjects and the deceased. The people saw the king's rule as a divine right, which later became known as The Mandate of Heaven, and although this mandate was established during the Zhou Dynasty its origins come from the Shang Dynasty.

The Zhou Dynasty

The last king of the Shang Dynasty was Zhou. Around 1,046 BCE, King Wu of the state of Zhou campaigned against King Zhou and defeated his army at the Battle of Muye, thus establishing the Zhou Dynasty. The dynasty lasted from 1,046 to 226 BCE with the Western Zhou Period and the Eastern Zhou Period dividing it between 1,046 to 771 BCE and 771 to 226 BCE respectively. It was Zhou's younger brother the Duke of Zhou who cited the Mandate of Heaven because he believed the Shang rulers were no longer acting in accordance with Heaven's blessings and thus, through this dispute, did the Zhou rulers find a legitimate way to declare war on the Shang.

According to the Duke the Mandate of Heaven was the divine right to rule and govern the people in the best interests of both the people and the gods. When a ruler did not lead as required the Mandate of Heaven would no longer apply to him and so the gods – through the people – were allowed to topple any ruler. Furthermore, the Mandate of Heaven could only apply to one individual, the legitimate ruler of the country. This right to rule was to be passed along the family line from father to son but only if the child himself possessed the correct character needed to serve as king. Over the following centuries those attempting to seize power continuously manipulated this concept to their own advantage.

Chinese culture developed even further during the Zhou Dynasty, the population also increased and the borders expanded to new regions, writing was organized and metal work advanced to a new level. Some of the greatest philosophers and writers emerged, including Confucius, Lao Tzu, Mo Ti and Tao Chien and Sun Tzu – known as one of China's, if not history's, greatest military tacticians – lived during this time. All of these individuals lived during a period that is known as the Hundred Schools of Thought, and although the chariot was introduced while the Shang Dynasty was in power it was during the reign of the Zhou Dynasty that it became something much more suitable for warfare.

The Spring, Autumn, and The Warring States Period

Chinese history marks the time between 772 and 476 BCE as the Spring and Autumn Period. It is named after the *Spring and Autumn Annals,* which is a collection of chronicles that speak about the government; it is also the earliest source that tells of the legendary Sun Tzu.

This period in time is known as the ending of the Western Zhou Period, when the government moved the capital to Luoyang – in the modern-day Henan Province – and began the new era of the Eastern Zhou Period. It is here that some of the greatest Chinese thinkers emerged, with Taoism, Confucianism and Mohist philosophies introduced into the region. However, some areas took to separating themselves from the main government at Luoyang and declared independence in the hope of gaining political power.

This drive to break away from the main government gave rise to what is known as the Warring States Period, that ran between 476 and 221 BCE, when the seven states continuously fought each other as political unrest gained momentum. These states included Zhao, Yan, Chu, Qin, Wei, Han and Qi. All of them declared independency, but none of them acknowledged the right to the Mandate of Heaven, which was still in the possession of the Zhou State in Luoyang. Since all of them employed similar battle strategies, and had armies of similar strength, none was able to rise above the others. This is also partially due to a single individual by the name of Mo Ti, a philosopher and engineer who acted as a spy in each; he was loyal to none and readily provided intelligence to whomever he wished. His objective was to stop any one state from overpowering another so that they would all eventually give up and form a peace treaty. He desired an end to the wars and is seen by many in a historical context as a peacemaker, alas, Mo Ti did not succeed and sometime between 262 and 260 BCE, the state of Qin conquered Zhao at the Battle of Changping.

It was Shang Yang of Qin (d. 338 BCE) who initiated an extensive series of reforms including the Qin belief that victory should be the main objective at any cost. However, it is Sun

Tzu who is given credit for reorganizing military strategies and tactics in battle. Some scholars are divided as to whether it was Shang Yang or Sun Tzu who reformed the military, but it seems likely that Shang Yang was familiar with *The Art of War*, which is accredited to Sun Tzu. Before the reforms warfare was considered a gentleman's game where everyone played by the same rules, one did not wage war on the weak in fear of losing honor. Another example of this earlier code suggested that an army should not charge if the other side was not yet prepared, so generals would go so far as to allow enough time for their opponent to line up before attacking.

Shang encouraged the army to forgo these principles and win at any cost, principles, which when used at Changping, saw more than 450,000 people captured and then slaughtered. This allowed the Qin state to gain an advantage and dominate the others. It was King Ying Zheng who first employed these new military strategies, Shang's reforms also brought about the creation of a powerful army and new weapons fashioned from iron. Thus it was that Ying Zheng was able to conquer the rest of the states one by one, and in 221 BCE he united all of the seven states under his banner and declared himself Shi Huangdi, or the First Emperor of China.

The Qin Dynasty

With his declaration as First Emperor Shi Huangdi founded the Qin Dynasty, which lasted between 221 and 206 BCE, and although technically the fourth dynasty, the Qin Dynasty is recognised as the first Imperial Dynasty in Chinese history.

Shi Huangdi is famous for tearing down the fortified walls that once separated the various states and joining them together to create a single defensive structure that protected his territory from invading nomads. This defensive structure later became known as the Great Wall of China and it is important to note that the original wall built by the First Emperor was much smaller than the one that exists today. Later dynasties came and added to the wall, until it became a highly complex network of effective defensive systems. Shi Huangdi also made great contributions to society through the construction of roads, bridges and buildings. He expanded the borders, began the construction of the Grand Canal in southern China, reallocated lands and tried his best to act justly with the people.

Yet, despite the great building projects and his military victories, Shi Huangdi soon found himself being resented by the people due to his strict policies. Declaring that he possessed the Mandate of Heaven, the First Emperor banned all philosophies of the day except for Legalism, which had been put forward by Shang Yang. He burned all historical and philosophical books that did not reflect his family, the state, or Legalism. The people no longer had any freedom to speak against the beliefs he propagated and if a group of people spoke up against him they were quickly isolated and shunned by those under Shi Huangdi's command.

Toward the later part of his life, and seeking ways to gain immortality, the First Emperor began to concentrate more on his afterlife. He began the construction of a lavish palace and ordered 8,000 terracotta warriors to guard his final resting place. Ironically he consumed an elixir that instead of giving him eternal life actually ended it, historians generally accept that he died from mercury poisoning.

His eldest son was known to be headstrong, with his own advisors, hand picked from among the available officials at his service. Meanwhile Li Siu, a corrupt advisor, hid the

Emperor's death from everyone until he was able to change the name of the Emperor's heir from his eldest son to his youngest son, Hu Hai. Li Siu did this because he believed he could control the youngest son and influence his rule as he saw fit, his plot worked and Hu Hai became the Second Emperor. However, the dynasty quickly fell into ruin after the death of the First Emperor as the Second Emperor turned out to be corrupt, and the people began to revolt against him, leaving it to Liu Bang to overthrow the corrupt Qin dynasty and establish the Han Dynasty (206 BC – 220 AD) several years later.

The Rise of Liu Bang

With the collapse of the Qin Dynasty the country descended into chaos, but two generals – who became famous at this time – Liu Bang from Hanzhong and King Xiang Yu from Chu, fought tooth and nail to seize control of the throne while supporters flocked to the man they thought would emerge as the victor. Xiang Yu had gained a reputation as a fierce warrior when he fought against the Qin, similarly, Liu Bang had earned the title King of the Han after defeating the Qin. They were allies initially and acted as such when they found themselves in opposition to each other, signing the Treaty of Hong Canal, which briefly resulted in peace.

Xiang Yu proposed that they divide the country into two, where Chu would rule the east and Han would rule the west; however, Liu Bang did not want the country to be split and broke the truce by attacking Xiang Yu's armies. In 202 BCE they met at the Battle of Gaixia where Liu Bang's general was able to defeat the Chu army. Liu Bang declared himself emperor and later became known as Emperor Gaozu, when Xiang Yu saw this, that he was losing the battle, he committed suicide. The remaining members of his family were permitted to live and were given posts in the new government, an act that was not as unusual as it may seem, as Liu Bang was known for showing respect to his enemies and for reuniting the country. He was also able to secure peace by firstly expelling those tribes who had supported Xiang Yu during the war, and secondly by formalizing treaties with the other independent states that had opposed the Qin. Except for a short disruption from Wang Meng the Han Dynasty ruled the country successfully for the next four centuries.

The Han Dynasty

Under Emperor Gaozu the Han Dynasty made great strides in advancing culture, society and technology. China also began trading with the West and new technologies were discovered as a result of education and learning. While the Zhou Dynasty was the first to produce a written history of the country, the First Emperor had then gone one to destroy vast libraries of literature. Historians generally agree that the Han Dynasty was the first to again begin to write histories, since none existed at the time. The famous *Canon of Medicine* was compiled and became the first written medical text to emerge in China and while gunpowder had been introduced to the country long before, it was developed further during the Han Dynasty. The Chinese also produced paper and used advanced writing tools to write books that were put into libraries. The government established Confucianism as the state philosophy and it became so widespread that it is still used today to influence decisions made by the government. In contrast to the First Emperor, Gaozu did not ban other ideologies, which, not surprisingly, ultimately led to advancements in education and literature, also vast numbers of men were released from military duties because the country was not in a state of war, like it had been previously.

When the emperor died in 195 BCE his son Liu Ying took the throne and continued with his father's policies to ensure that the country enjoyed a long period of stability. Out of all the Han emperors, Wu Ti was the one who took the country through one of the greatest moments in Chinese history. During Wu Ti's rule the borders were expanded, public buildings were created and new inventions were made. In 138 CE he sent Zhang Qian west to build trade routes, and the Silk Road was finished eight years later. Confucianism was officially taught in schools as part of the government curriculum so that young adults would emerge with insight into the ideology that had become so crucial to Chinese culture. Transportation and trading networks were improved, the economy grew and thousands of people were able to gain employment.

The Fall of Han and the Rise of the Xin Dynasty

In the 9th century CE Wang Mang overthrew the Han rulers, seized the throne and claimed the Mandate of Heaven for himself. He had planned and plotted his rise because he wanted to redistribute wealth among the peasants and the nobility. This was the foundation of Xin Dynasty, which lasted between 9 and 23 CE. Of course the peasants initially supported him, but the landowners disliked his policies and despite his best intentions the policies he strove to establish were not properly thought out and unemployment – along with resentment – soon spread across the land. Adding to his troubles the Yellow River once more brought misery and destruction through floods, and so it was – as the rebels organized uprisings – that Wang Mang was slain by very the same peasants he had overthrown the previous government for.

The Xin Dynasty's rise marked the end of what is regarded as the Western Han period, but when only a few years later the Xin Dynasty itself fell – and with the Han rulers reinstated – the Eastern Han period is seen as having begun. The new emperor gave the previous landowners their lands back and brought peace to what had become a chaotic period, but even though the old policies were reinstated the emperor constantly found himself trying to prevent uprisings in what are now known as Korea and Vietnam. Although he tried his best to ensure that the regions remained under Chinese rule, the Vietnamese Trưng sisters, for instance, led a revolt against the Chinese in 40 CE, forcing China to send tens of thousands troops to subdue the rebels.

Guang Wu was able to consolidate his authority in these areas and the borders were expanded once more, with the resulting increase in trade. When Emperor Zhang took the throne in 75 CE, the empire had amassed a great deal of wealth, with revenue coming from the extensive trading that was conducted between the Chinese and other civilizations such as the Roman Empire. Marcus Aurelius was a Roman Emperor who believed that silk was priceless, and so he gave the Chinese traders whatever price they asked for. As a result, China took great advantage of other nations to build its economy during this time.

Despite the increase in prosperity there were still some squabbles between the rich landowners and the peasantry, a period that is referred to as the Five Pecks of Rice Rebellion and the Yellow Turban Rebellions of 184 CE. The nature of the first rebellion was religious to begin with, but over time things changed. The rebellion attracted lots of peasants who were in opposition to the Confucian policies set by the emperor. The government did not possess the power to suppress these rebellions and experienced a major insurgence. General Cao Cao and General Yuan Shao fought against the government and then turned on each other as they both attempted to seize power, and although Cao Cao won the battle, he lost to the southern warlords at the famous Battle of Red Cliffs in 208 CE. This battle is known to be one of the largest naval battles in history, and the result once more resulted in the empire being divided, this time into three kingdoms known as Shu, Wei and Wu.

The period that followed came to be known as the Three Kingdoms era and although the Shu, Wei and Wu kingdoms were the main players, several other dynasties briefly emerged. These include the Jin and the Wei Dynasties that existed between 208 and 618 CE; however, it was the Sui Dynasty (589 – 618 CE) that reunited the country once more. The Sui Dynasty is known for using effective government strategies that did not upset the peasants – unlike those of many of the previous rulers.

During the reigns of Emperors Wen and Yang, China saw sections of the Great Wall repaired and lengthened, while the Grand Canal was expanded to such an extent that it became the longest artificial waterway in the world. The army enlisted so many new recruits that it became the largest the world had ever seen. Poetry and literature advanced to new levels and many works were published that spread far and wide, of particular note is the tale of Hua Mulan – that many people outside of China now know through the animation released by Disney in 1998. The story tells of a young woman who secretly takes her father's position within the army and creates mischievous havoc, the tale is still related to young children today.

Despite these worthy achievements both emperors continually looked towards Korea for extra land and resources. Emperor Wen had become so obsessed with warfare that he had drained the national treasury to build fortifications and to fund his military campaigns. By the time Emperor Wen's rule came to an end the people were fed up with government spending. When Emperor Yang tried to use the people's wealth to fund military campaigns against Korea in a similar fashion, he was assassinated in a coup orchestrated by Yuwen Huaji in 618 CE. After that, Li Yuan – the first cousin of Emperor Yang – rose with his followers to take the throne. He was renamed Emperor Gao Tzu whereupon he founded the Tang Dynasty.

The Tang Dynasty

The Tang Dynasty ran from 618 to 907 CE and this time period is often referred to as China's Golden Era. The emperor continued running the government as it had been done previously, but with some improvements, for one he stopped spending money on massive building projects and unnecessary military campaigns, because he was wise enough not repeat his predecessor's mistakes.

Unfortunately his son, Li Shimin – who also murdered his siblings and several individuals in the aristocracy – assassinated him in 626 CE. He declared himself Emperor Taizhong and ordered Buddhist temples to be erected where the dead had fallen in battle. He claimed the Mandate of Heaven had been given to him and that whomever he had slain would become his advisor in the afterlife. Despite the fact that he usurped his way to the throne he proved himself to be a capable emperor and was skilled in military tactics and this is probably why he was not challenged by any warlords or assassinated like so many of his predecessors.

Emperor Taizhong continued running the country using much the same policies that had popularized the Sui Dynasty's government, a fact we can particularly see through his new legal codes, which he borrowed greatly from Sui ideas. He was critical of weak punishments for specific crimes and felt that the punishments should be harsher. In contrast to his father he disregarded a static foreign policy and allowed a succession of military campaigns to take place that expanded the Chinese borders.

The Silk Road, more prosperous than ever before, resulted in business links to the West being strengthened and even though the Roman Empire had fallen due to its own wars, the Byzantine Empire was very much supportive of the silk trade. In 712 CE, when Emperor Xuanzong came to power, China was the wealthiest and most populous civilization in the world. The government was able to build an army of epic proportions, which was strong enough to crush both internal and external threats. During the Tang Dynasty the art, science and technology fields developed even further, and many sculptures – including those depicting Chinese ancestors – were carved during this time.

The Descent of Tang and the Ascent of the Sung Dynasty

Despite the amazing achievements that came about during the Tang Dynasty, there still existed resentment towards the government and various rebellions occurred. In 755 CE the An Lushan Rebellion broke out causing the death of thousands of people. An Lushan was a general and much-loved by the imperial court, but after poisoning the minds of the people at court, he staged a revolt against the government. He led more than 100,000 men in a military coup and announced that he was the new emperor. In 763 CE An Lushan was overthrown but the damage had already been done, a series of other uprisings occurred through a kind of domino effect and masses of people were killed.

Due to these continuous and bloody revolts the population decreased dramatically and witnessed a steep decline, scholars have estimated that anywhere between 13 to 36,000,000 people died from internal revolts alone. Because trading networks were diminished and taxes were not being collected, the Imperial Court abandoned the capital at Chang'an and headed for safety elsewhere and after another rebellion occurred between 874 and 884 CE, the Tang Dynasty began to decline. In 907 CE the dynasty collapsed completely and splintered off into various states, all of which declared that they were the legitimate dynasty. This period is known as the Five Dynasties and the Ten Kingdoms Period (907 – 960 CE) and China remained divided until the founding of the Sung or Song Dynasty (960 – 1279 CE).

During the Song Dynasty a state of stability finally began to reestablish itself once more, new laws, organizations and practices were introduced to create a more just society. Neo-Confucianism had become the main philosophy that went on to influence all aspects of government and culture, however, the usual state of conflict between the affluent landowners and the peasantry continued. One could say they even continue today, because the poor are unhappy with their low wages and lack of rights, and the rich continue to get richer and seemingly command all that they see.

Chapter 3 – European and Russian History

Early Middle Ages (475 – 1000 CE)

As stated in Chapter One, Rome had begun to face a series of invasions of Germanic tribes from the 3rd century onwards, and her generals – those who went on to become emperors – were quickly assassinated by those seeking the same position and power. This carried on until Constantine's time, when he made great religious reforms with the promotion of Christianity. Theodosius I established Christianity again as the new religion in the 4th century, but there were continuous raids and invasions from the Goths, Gauls and the Sassanids from the eastern regions, and the Huns also caused the Goths to migrate eastwards into Roman territory, which triggered fighting between the two. When Theodosius I died, the Eastern Roman Empire collapsed, and was later reorganized into what became known as the Byzantine Empire. In 410-455 CE Rome was besieged by the Germanic king Odovacar, a man who brought about the end of the last emperor of the Western Roman Empire and thus the Roman Empire itself.

Emperor Justinian reigned from 527 to 565 CE and attempted to take back the territory that once belonged to the Roman Empire, including parts of North Africa, Italy and modern-day France. While he seemed to succeed at first he could not maintain control over these regions. The campaigns were far too expensive and the Byzantine Empire faced incursions from the Lombards, who were seeking territory in Italy. As a result the empire was unable to hold on to any gains below south of Italy. At the turn of the 7th century CE the Byzantine Empire held a small strip of North Africa, Parts of Egypt, Anatolia,

Thrace, the Balkans and the Levant. Modern-day Germany and France were in the hands of the Franks, while the Visigoths possessed the majority of the Iberian Peninsula or modern-day Spain. Britain, known as Britannia at the time, was held by the Angles, and the Saxons controlled Denmark.

The foundations of medieval Europe were laid down between 600 and 800 CE, just as the Byzantine Empire faced the full strength of the Avars, who were making their way towards Thrace. Furthermore, the Sassanids of Persia were able to take the Levant and Anatolia, and although Heraclius eventually defeated the Sassanids the damage had already been done. The empire was drained from constant warfare and was left severely weakened. At this time Islamic forces moved in and removed the Byzantine Empire's influence from all regions except Anatolia. Since the Byzantine Empire was now in such a precarious position, placed between the Avars and the Islamic armies, the Christian rulers looked to take back the Middle East by force. To them the Middle East was the birthplace of their Christian faith, and such was their intent to conquer them that they ignored most of their responsibilities back in their own homelands.

Italy was divided up into various regions held by a number of tribes including the Lombards, who had formed an uneasy relationship with other rulers. France was divided between the Franks, Visigoths and the Burgundians before the establishment of the Merovingian dynasty, which was made up of Clovis and his heirs. Their descendants – who tried to gain as much power as possible – further divided these territories, this internal fighting over thrones, and the armies assembled, were just two reasons why any ruler could not survive the chaos. Furthermore, any provincial government only controlled the outer areas with the military forces that were available. Because there were so many power struggles happening between the rulers and their relatives, the guards of the palace were given strict orders to initiate a full lockout whenever a king died.

It was Pepin II who reunited the Franks – by suppressing the rebels throughout the Merovingian territory – and Charles Martel continued his father's work by taking control of the eastern regions and fighting the Islamic forces in 732 CE. Pepin III, the son of Charles Martel, overthrew the last Merovingian king with the backing of the Church. His reputation grew to such a degree that he was also asked to defeat the Lombards in Italy who had created fear among the population. In 752 Pope Stephen II awarded Pepin III with the title Protector of the Romans. The Church was able to expand its powers through its priests in the outer regions and created Papal States during the 10th century.

His son, Carlos Magnus, in turn reigned as Charlemagne from 768 to 814 CE and began the Carolingian dynasty. The headquarters for this dynasty were located in the center of modern day France and he was able to rally against the Saxons in what we know as Germany today, it was also a time when many people converted to Catholicism. He was able to take Catholicism into modern day Poland, the Czech Republic, Bohemia and other areas. In 800 Charlemagne was declared the Holy Roman Emperor but, as history continually shows, his heirs continued to squabble amongst themselves after he died.

During the 9th century there was a sharp decline in the Carolingian Empire when the Vikings and the Normans launched raids in Italy, Spain and France. Also, the Islamic navy had established centers in Sicily, northwest France and

Apulia. It was at Sicily and Apulia that the Normans were able to defeat the Islamic invaders, which historians believe to be the origin of the Crusades. These developments caused the Europeans to remobilize and reconsider their surroundings while the idea of feudalism appeared and explained the individual bond between vassals. Bishops provided ethical supervision, justice and management of law to help build a more orderly society.

From the early 7th century the Church extended its political hierarchy and broke away from Constantinople, as there was now a difference between the doctrines of the Church and those that were being taught in the capital. Monasticism emerged and stimulated the Church to grow and expand, these new reforms originated in the Middle East during the 9th and 10th centuries. The Church wanted to continue traditional lessons and reduce the amount of hostilities throughout the continent, but at the same time still encourage the taking back of the Middle East from Islamic forces. Monks became new popes and the Church was able to gain a strong foothold in Europe.

The intricate political chaos experienced throughout Europe started to simplify during the mid-tenth century when the post-Carolingian upper classes chose Conrad and Henry I as new kings, those duchies that refused to hand over power were overthrown. Ruling between 936 and 973 CE Otto I overthrew the duchies in the eastern regions and defeated the Magyars in 955 CE in the area known today as Hungary. He attacked the Slavs and was successful in conquering them, such that the Slavs changed their religion and became Christians, he was named Emperor in 996 CE with the approval of his cousin Pope Gregory V; all the while the spiritual and political influence of the Church continued to expand. At the same time, medieval France was controlled by the Carolingians who had spun a complex web of feudal duchies to suit their rule. Hugh Capet was declared king in 987 but only came to rule over a reduced kingdom.

Elsewhere Islamic forces laid siege to Constantinople, while Byzantine struggled to hold them off, forced into uneasy relationships with the kingdoms surrounding it. Orthodox Christianity was established, which was totally independent of some of the doctrines taught by the Church because the Byzantine Empire administered all matters that were religious in nature. It also played an active role in developing the details of creed and specific doctrines, which can be seen from the Iconoclastic controversies that occurred in the middle of the 9th century.

During the 9th century the Byzantine Empire suffered various hardships but in the 10th century it experienced a revival, but this was primarily due to the fact that the Muslims experienced political chaos themselves. The Byzantine Empire was victorious over the Bulgars with the leadership of Basil II – who reigned between 963 and 1025 CE – here the armies gathered and descended upon the Islamic forces to recover both Cyprus and Crete. In 1054 the Byzantine Empire and Europe were finally divided between those who believed in Catholicism and those who favored the Orthodox faiths. That same year the empire found itself at war with tribes from modern day Turkey and before there was any time to seek aid from the Church, the empire had fallen.

Political Struggle during the Middle Ages (920 – 1250 CE)

By the early 10th century the Carolingian dynasty had run its course and the Vikings had created settlements of their own throughout Western Europe. In the east, the Magyars controlled the region, and in North Africa the Fatimids were in power. Hugh Capet was elected king of France in 987 CE, but he was considered to be weak by the feudal nobles and here it is important to note that the king and his heirs were expected to act in accordance with the feudal organization; however, the king used these concepts for his own interests instead. He was ambitious and won various lands through political influence and warfare.

At the end of the 11th century Louis VI had enough power to dominate the feudal lords in both title and in strength. His successor, Louis VII, faced the Angevin Empire, which was governed by the Plantagenets. In 1066 William the Bastard defeated King Harold's English forces at Hasting's and subjected Anglo-Saxon culture to that of the Normans. Since the Angevin Empire had ties through marriage with its enemies, it was considered to be dangerous by the French kings. In 1214 at the Battle of Bouvines, Philip II Augustus met Otto IV and John of England in battle and was able to conquer them. John returned to England full of shame and was forced to sign the Magna Carta. Louis IX ruled France well and gained a reputation as a wise leader.

What is now modern day Germany was once a formidable kingdom during the mid-10th and mid-11th centuries. Feudalism had been banned from the reign of Otto I, and the German king – defeating the Magyars in 955 at Lechfield – continued to rule since he had control over the Church. This allowed him to effectively bypass the nobles and their demands and in 962 he became the next Holy Roman Emperor, while his sons Otto II and Otto III followed in his footsteps, all of whom appointed various Popes, bypassed the nobles and supported new reforms within the Church. Papal reforms occurred in the monasteries that pushed the belief that only the Pope should be allowed to make decisions concerning Church matters. These new tensions – that became prevalent during the reign of Henry IV and Gregory VII – ultimately caused the Papal-German Investiture Controversy.

Controversy saw the emperor overthrown and the Pope kidnapped, an act that was to see him eventually die amongst the Normans. During the early 12th century European rulers were forced to accept the Pope as the sole authority who assigned high prelates, the very representative of God on earth; however, the rulers did possess the power to place sanctions upon the high prelates if they had enough evidence, but on the turning of the 12th century, the Church had enough influence and command to put forth a crusade to take back the Holy Land.

When the Byzantine Empire was suffering from internal deterioration and decay, the Seljuk Turks were able to conquer the remnants of any resistance in 1071 at Manzikert, and as a result Asia Minor was left to Turkish rule. Meanwhile, the Orthodox Church had broken away from the Catholic Church and was in danger. In 1096 the First Crusade was launched, it lasted for three years and resulted in Christian forces taking back control of Jerusalem and also led to the establishment of a series of Crusader States under the feudal nobles. In 1147 the Second Crusade was set under way but was ultimately unsuccessful and after a very decisive battle in 1197, the Holy Land fell to Salah al-Din al-Ayyubi. From 1189 onwards the Third Crusade began and ended after two years without anything to show for all that was sacrificed in terms of money, men and time. The Fourth Crusade, beginning in 1202, also lasted for two years and also resulted in failure, primarily due to the infighting among the Frankish and Venetian leaders. Instead, they sacked Constantinople and founded states for the Byzantine king to return.

Disagreements with the Church had caused the German kings to become significantly weakened and it was only with the ascension of Frederick I Barbarossa – in 1152 – that the German monarchs began a revival during the Hohenstaufen dynasty. Frederick I Barbarossa managed to convince the feudal nobles to appoint him as their feudal overlord and for the most part was able to secure their allegiance. Frederick I Barbarossa initially travelled to Italy to help the Popes but there found himself in the middle of Church succession disagreements. When he tried to make decisions, both the Church and the local towns reacted by warring against him, working together they defeated him in 1176 at Legnano. Frederick I Barbarossa died during the Third Crusade in 1190.

By marrying into the House of Norman his son, Frederick II, became king of both Sicily and Germany in 1215. He had a reputation of being a highly educated man but was opposed by both Italy and the Church, this was because he had dare postpone the next Crusade that the Church had wanted to launch, and so he was effectively left isolated. In 1229 he finally began making his way to the Holy Land with his army where, surprisingly, he was able to take control of the Holy Land through negotiation instead of war. Yet, because he did not actually fight, Pope Innocent IV excommunicated him. Throughout the remainder of his rule both Italy and the Church plotted against Frederick II. In 1244 Jerusalem came under Western control for the final time, since the Khwarazmshah armies were attacked by the Mongolians. In what is now modern day Spain the Castilian kings managed to control nearly two thirds of the country while sacrilegious activities in France gradually diminished.

Renaissance

After the Middle Ages Europe experienced the Renaissance, – a cultural movement that began in Italy – it was a time that witnessed the arrival of humanism, a new way of thinking that became manifest in art, architecture, politics, science and literature. The early promoters of this new philosophy, including Francesco Petrarch, drew inspiration from ancient Greek and Roman works. It was a combination of ideas from Plato and Socrates with only some concepts derived from Catholicism, but because this philosophy was so comprehensively pushed forward, the fields of art and literature went through considerable change.

The Renaissance was born in Italy but it quickly paved a wide path throughout Europe. Many Italian politicians, officials and merchants were great supporters of the artists and provided financial support when necessary, with many great houses and estates decorated with impressive pieces of art. Out of all the city-states the strongest and most influential were Milan, Florence, Venice and the ones under the direction of the Pope.

The different states all had their own unique characteristics, mainly because they had their own specific forms of government ruling over them. The Renaissance is generally accepted amongst scholars to have been initiated in Florence where merchants grew rich by trading wool. The city remained wealthy throughout many years because of the influential Medici family, one that, on the whole, ran the state and maintained the city's finances wisely.

In Rome the Pope ruled both the state and the Church, and so it was that the Pope effectively became an international politician and intermediary between the rulers of the various city-states. It is said by some scholars that many popes became corrupted because of their intervention in worldly matters, when they should have been solely focused on Church governance. Rome, which had suffered tremendously during the Middle Ages, became increasingly progressive because of the Renaissance.

Milan and Venice became incredibly wealthy cities during the Renaissance and contributed greatly to politics, so it wasn't at all surprising that artists from all over the world found themselves attracted to these beautiful cities. In either place an artist could find wealthy patrons who would commission a variety of artworks from them, also a number of writers found inspiration amongst the beauty and wealth they exhibited.

Giotto is known as one of the most famous painters from the early Renaissance period, and Ghiberti's work on creating new perception was revolutionary in the sculpting world. Other artists like Donatello and Botticelli refined these methods through further development. New inventions like the world had never seen came about during the latter part of this time period, referred to as the High Renaissance. Some of the greatest artists including Michelangelo, Raphael, and Leonardo da Vinci appeared and created works that are still famous to this day, and will undoubtedly remain so for as long as they exist. The printing press was invented, which allowed literature and art to become an integral part of daily life, at last accessible to the masses. Some of the greatest writers of the day including Niccolò Machiavelli, Pico and Boccaccio, now had the tools available to distribute their writings and share their ideas easily.

As great as the Renaissance was, there were the inevitable events that would lead to its demise. To begin with, in 1494, the French invaded Italy; this was the result of a culmination of European powers for years having been focused on the prize of Italy. Foreigners sacked Rome in 1527, and during the reign of the Holy Roman Emperor Charles V the Renaissance finally came to its end. Charles V implemented a number of measures that limited economic progression and the Church, fearful of the new ideas and freedoms the movement of the Renaissance had brought, also set about imposing strict penalties that eventually became law. Italy was no longer the center of the greatest artistic age the world had ever seen.

Nonetheless, a number of famous inventions were made during this time. In the 15th century, Leonardo da Vinci created the robotic knight, which can be considered to be the first mechanical robot. It was made in the form of armor in which a complex gear and pulley mechanism was contained; the knight was put on display for the people to see at a party held by the Duke of Milan. In the early 16th century Andrea Amati invented the violin, and although something similar to the violin existed before his time, Amati is known to have created the first to have four strings and modern violins, though based on his work, are actually much larger than the ones he originally made. In 1643 Evangelista Torricelli invented the barometer to measure air pressure, this invention, incorporated into modern thermostatic technology, is still used today.

Napoleonic Europe

By the end of the 18th century Europe had seen the French Revolution give way to the Thermidorian Reaction. It was now that one of the greatest European military leaders stamped his mark on history. In 1799 Napoleon Bonaparte was elected head of the Consulate and led France to become one of the superpowers of the day. Under Napoleon the French crushed domestic uprisings, seized lands within Italy and campaigned against other nations. In 1801 Napoleon forged new relationships with the Church and restructured the laws in France through the Napoleonic Code. Three years later Napoleon had amassed enough power to declare himself Emperor of the French.

Napoleon grew stronger with each victory, European powers kept attacking him, one after the other, but all were defeated. He won Marengo in 1800, with other victories five and seven years later, and in 1807 Czar Alexander I found himself with no choice but to forge an alliance with him by signing the Treaty of Tilsit. Napoleon went on to establish numerous states that were loyal to him and eventually had control over much of Europe. The ideas of the French Revolution influenced anyone who met him or had a discussion with him. The only battle he lost – before his final defeat in 1815 – was the Battle of Trafalgar against the British navy, which occurred on 21st October 1805.

Britain was one of a few countries that posed a threat to Napoleon, so to tackle this he imposed the Continental System in 1806. It was intended to prevent Britain from being able to trade with the rest of Europe but the plan backfired and Napoleon instead faced the consequences. Firstly, German nationalism began to take root due to the very ideas evoked by the French Emperor. Secondly, the Continental System resulted in the Peninsular War in Spain, which caused the French army have to divert essential resources away from the rest of the continent.

Napoleon's wife Josephine was abandoned in 1810 because she had not given him a child and he replaced her with the younger Marie Louise of Austria, together, they produced a son who they planned to call the King of Rome. For a time they were a happy family until the Russian Czar pulled Russia out of the Continental System in 1810. Two years later Napoleon began marching on Moscow and while he was able to push the Russians further and further into their homeland, the bitter cold of the winter crippled his forces. Napoleon withdrew so he could assemble a stronger force, but the following year he was defeated by a coalition of European powers at the Battle of Leipzig.

In 1814 Napoleon fell into disgrace and was exiled to Elba Island during the coronation of Louis XVIII. The new king was Bourbon, which meant that he was from the same dynastic line that had lost the throne two decades before. Just as Louis XVIII was arranging a new agreement with the other European powers, Napoleon fled Elba Island and returned to France to mobilize a new army, a period referred to as the Hundred Days. In 1815 Napoleon faced Blucher and Wellington on the Battlefields of Waterloo where he was once and for all finally defeated. Exiled to Saint Helena he eventually died there, a tiny isolated place with no accolades or glory.

At the hands of Napoleon Europe had suffered nearly twenty years of bloodshed and chaos, his defeat and exile brought a desperate need for Europe to be reconciled. A great meeting known as the Congress of Vienna was arranged between the European powers; Austria, Russia, France, Britain and Prussia met to negotiate and secure a peaceful and stable continent. The goal was to ensure that one country would never again be able to overpower any other, just as France had done for so many years. The Congress of Vienna was – for a time successful – because this mutual agreement brought relative peace to the continent; that was until the horrors of the First World War once more threw Europe into darkness.

The February Revolution

In 1917 the Russian Revolution took place, with one of its first stages commonly referred to as the February Revolution. The revolution burst into flame because an increasing number of the Russian common people had lost confidence in the leadership of Tsar Nicholas II and looked to remove him from power. There was a succession of bloody demonstrations and uprisings in Petrograd, known today as St. Petersburg. The people were unhappy at the state of the economy, the scarcity of food and supplies, Russia's disastrous involvement in the First World War, and all-in-all simply wished for change.

While Petrograd supported the February Revolution, the rest of the population may not have condoned either it or its instigators; however, the newly installed provisional regime was certainly more democratic than the monarchy it had replaced and the interests of the people were now perhaps at last being taken into consideration.

The October Revolution

Also known as the Bolshevik Revolution, the October Revolution toppled the new provisional regime and led to the foundation of the Soviet Union. This time the rebels were far more organized than before because they were arranged into smaller groups. Bolsheviks led the revolution after planning extensively for six-months, but when they first introduced themselves in 1917, they were not on the whole very popular with the Russian population. Yet, by the end of the year they had gained considerable support from the people due to the promises they had made, garnering support from the urban centers of Petrograd and other large cities.

By the end of 1917 the Bolsheviks finally came to realize that they simply could not hold onto power without an elected government, if, that is, they wished to continue refusing to share the mechanisms of rule. In January 1918 they abandoned democracy and declared themselves to be the leaders of a proletariat dictatorship, this was the exact reason so many people had revolted earlier, because they did not want a dictatorship, so as a result the country was soon plunged into the Russian Civil War that waged until 1920.

English Civil War

During the mid-17th century, England, Scotland and Ireland were sparsely populated and the people had been subjected to any incidences of prolonged warfare within their kingdoms. To them the outbreak of a regional skirmish may have been little more than an inconvenience, but what began as a series of disagreements between King Charles I and the English Parliament developed into a fully mobilized armed struggle, one that took the lives of an estimated 800,000 people, primarily in Ireland where around 600,000 died due to famine, illness and disease.

The English Civil Wars were fueled by conflicts in Scotland and Ireland that had developed in the preceding years. The Bishops' Wars in Scotland and the Ulster Rebellion in Ireland had further increased the tension between Charles I and Parliament and although the Civil War destroyed England beyond comprehension, it also devastated the other two kingdoms held by the House of Stuart. For this reason, the English Civil Wars can readily be called the Wars of the Three Stuart Kingdoms.

The first English Civil War was fought between 1642 and 1646, while the second began in 1648 and resulted in the shocking execution of the king. The third war took place between 1649 and 1651, where one side supported the Royals and the other supported Parliament, the king, forced to flee, gave momentum to the idea that initiated the establishment of the Commonwealth of England. It was a government that was heavily influenced by a political and military expert named Oliver Cromwell. The New Model Army's victory over the king's forces forever changed the English constitution, with the new roles of both the monarchy and parliament creating a considerable shift in politics across the British Isles.

The wars ultimately broke out because there was an attempt to unify the three countries. In 1603 the line of the Tudors came to an end because Queen Elizabeth I died without any heirs apparent, the throne, therefore, was passed to her cousin King James VI of Scotland, who became King James I of England and Ireland. This marked the beginning of power for the Stuarts and for the very first time, the three kingdoms of England, Ireland and Scotland were united under one monarch. King James I had great difficulty in maintaining peace across these kingdoms because there was a long and bloody history of conflict between them. Many had hatred towards the neighboring kingdoms and animosity had eaten into each society, civil war seemed inevitable.

The three kingdoms had differing views on the role of the monarchy and the state. James I had a lot of power and freedom to do as he wished when he was the King of Scotland, he was able to command the Scottish parliament and ruled with little criticism, but these powers were heavily restricted heavily when he took the English throne. Here he had limited access to the treasury, which upset him greatly, because known as an extravagant king, James was constantly short of funds and became frustrated by Parliament's refusal to give in to his demands.

Furthermore, the three kingdoms had a different dominant religion. The English were predominantly Protestant, the Scottish were Calvinist and the Irish were primarily Catholic. There were also a number of influential religious minorities within each kingdom that further complicated this precarious melting pot of faith.

Before becoming the King of England and Ireland, James had promised to adopt a tolerant stance on religion by stating that he would not persecute anyone unless they broke the law. However, James did not keep his promise. He persecuted the English Catholics when he became king just as severely as he had done before, so in 1605 – disillusioned by James' false promises and determined to be heard – a group of Catholic conspirators orchestrated the famous Gunpowder Plot. The conspirators were led by a man named Robert Catesby who planned to blow up the Houses of Parliament with King James inside. However, evidence of gunpowder and matches was found before they could carry out the bombing, and with the authorities eventually discovering the plotters Catesby was killed during a gun battle. The plot ended up being a failure and Catesby's head was set on a spike outside the Houses of Parliament as a reminder to anyone who plotted against the king.

Despite the dramatic events of 1605 James' reign was a time of relative peace across the three kingdoms because James had done his best to keep his recently united kingdoms out of foreign conflicts. However, in the later years of his reign,

James unwittingly dragged England, Scotland and Ireland into what became the Thirty Years' War. The war took place from 1618 to 1648 and was one of the deadliest wars to ever occur in Europe. Historians believe it was the tension between the Protestants, Catholics and Calvinists that fueled the war, with each religious group having formed its own league they all looked to gain power over the others.

In 1625 King James I of England died and his second son, King Charles I, ascended to the throne. In the early years of his rule Charles succeeded in alienating many of his peers and subjects. Already an unpopular figure, with a reputation for being severe and arrogant, Charles inherited the Duke of Buckingham as his principal Minister. If Charles was unpopular in Parliament, then the Duke of Buckingham was practically detested. Unfortunately Charles did not inherit his father's desire for peace and – under instruction from Buckingham – he threw his kingdoms whole-heartedly into the ongoing fight against the Catholic forces.

As time passed Charles became steadily more unpopular with his subjects across all three of the kingdoms he ruled. To generate income Charles resorted to reviving a tax that had not been seen since the Elizabethan times. The "ship money" levy was an annual tax on seaports and coastal towns that was collected to pay for the Royal Navy. In 1635 Charles applied this tax to inland towns and began collecting from any citizen who had the means to pay. Parliament and tax-paying citizens were shocked at what they considered to be an illegal tax imposed by the king. In the same year Charles introduced a series of ecclesiastical reforms in England and Charles' Queen Henrietta Maria of France was openly Catholic at court. So was William Laud, who was the close adviser of Charles and the archbishop of Canterbury. This led many English

Protestants, including the more zealous puritans, to become suspicious of an increase in "popery" in England, and feared that Charles was trying to restore the Catholic faith.

At first it seemed that Charles had only a few supporters, with the majority of the English nobility and landed gentry reluctant to pledge allegiance so early in the war, but there were those who believed in the "Divine Right of Kings" and supported Charles' innovations in the Church. On the other hand, Charles had alienated many with his actions in the Thirty Years' War because he had applied taxes that had left the citizens in despair and as such Parliament felt that he had betrayed the Protestant Church. The ruling classes were effectively split down the middle and thus so was the stage set for the first English Civil War.

Chapter 4– American History

Native Americans

The story of Native Americans begins thousands of years before the Europeans set off across the wide stretch of ocean to discover a great "unknown" continent. North America was actually colonized by a group of people who left Asia when they crossed over a now submerged land bridge from modern day Siberia and reached today's Alaska around twelve thousand years ago. These settlers were the ancestors of the First Nation peoples whom the Europeans came across several centuries ago.

The initial settlers who trekked from Asia consisted of only a few thousand. When the Europeans arrived in North America, the native population had grown much larger. There is some dispute among scholars as to the exact number but it is estimated that between 7 and 18 million natives were present in North America before European colonization. Other studies show that around 10 million natives lived in the region that is now considered to be the United States of America.

Over time these settlers quickly spread across the eastern-southern regions and established themselves on the new land. Archaeologists and anthropologists have separated the continent into separate regions, where different groups of natives practiced similar customs and lifestyles. Academics have divided North America into ten areas: the Plateau, the Northwest Coastal region, the Great Basin, the Plains, California, the Southeast, the Southwest, the Northeast, the Subarctic and the Arctic regions. It is important to note that Mexico is not included in this classification.

The Arctic

Technically a frozen desert the Arctic region is a freezing flat area close to the Arctic Circle in modern day Greenland, Alaska and Canada. It is the homeland of the Aleut and the Inuit who speak a language that originated from the Eskimo-Aleut language family. The population of the Arctic is relatively smaller than other culture regions due to the unwelcoming landscape, and those that do live here are spread across a vast region. The natives of these lands were nomadic in nature and followed the polar bears, seals and other animals as they travelled throughout the tundra. The Aleut were more settled in the southern regions and had established fishing centers along the coastline.

Both the Aleut and the Inuit shared various customs and practices, with both typically fashioning houses in the shape of domes made from wood or turf, or from ice in the northern regions. The fur from seals and otters was used to make warm and waterproof clothes while they also built elongated open-aired boats and used dogsleds to travel across the ice-bound land. In 1867, after the United States bought Alaska, the consequences of what the native population had suffered became apparent. Through disease, death and oppression, the Inuit and the Aleut only had a remaining population of 2500. Today, the descendants of those who survived continue to live in the region.

The Subarctic

The subarctic region is mostly comprised of Canada, inland Alaska and the tundra. The region features swampy pine forests known as taiga with those who live in the subarctic region separated into distinctive two language groups. The first are known as the Algonquian speakers found in the east, which include the Naskapi, the Ojibwa and the Cree. The second are Athabaskan speakers in the west, which include the Deg Xinag, the Kuchin and the Tsattine.

Travelling across this region has always been extremely challenging and those who travelled frequently used kayaks, snowshoes and toboggans. The population here is much lower than in other cultural regions and is widely scattered across the territory. Most of the population stayed in family units instead of forming larger, stable settlements and lived in portable tents and structures that could be transported as they followed the caribou herds. When the weather grew too cold to live in tents, they created warmer shelters by digging trenches.

During the 1600s and the 1700s the fur trade grew dramatically and had a deep impact on the lifestyle of the nomadic families who lived in the region. The natives relied on hunting to feed themselves and their families. As time passed they began to rely ever more heavily on trading furs with the early European settlers to survive, unfortunately this led to local societies being displaced and many were wiped out by diseases that Europeans introduced to the local populations as they had no natural immunity against them.

The Northeast

The Northeast Culture was one of the earliest cultures that interacted with the newly arrived Europeans. This culture lived along today's Atlantic coastline, all the way from Canada to North Carolina in the United States, even reaching as far as the Mississippi River. The people who lived in this area were also divided into two key groups: the Algonquian speakers that lived along the coastline, and the Iroquoian speakers who settled near the riverbanks and lakes. The Algonquian included the Delaware, Shawnee, Fox, Pequot and the Menominee peoples, whereas the Iroquoian included the

Tuscarora, Seneca, Erie, Oneida, and the Cayuga peoples. The Algonquian had a larger population but the Iroquoians, living in permanent settlements, did not have to periodically move to survive.

The Iroquoians were very aggressive in nature and they would continuously raid those they hadn't formed ties with, their raids only increased with the arrival of the Europeans. Although it was difficult to do so, the First Nation peoples were forced to set their differences aside to fight against the European newcomers. The Europeans were smart and in many cases attempted to make the natives fight each other instead. As more Europeans arrived and made their way west, the peoples, who had lived for millennia off the land now being colonized, began to dwindle even further.

The Southeast

Stretching between the northern area of the Gulf of Mexico and just south of the Northeast region, the Southeast possessed a lush and warm area suitable for agriculture. The majority of the peoples who lived in this region were skilled farmers who created small but thriving communities referred to as hamlets, and they grew foods such as sunflowers, butternut squash, maize and tobacco. Out of all the people living in the Southeast region, the best known are probably the Seminole, Choctaw and the Cherokee. There is evidence to suggest that they spoke dialects belonging to the Muskogean language.

After the United States declared independence from the British Empire, most of the cultures living in this region were either killed off by disease or displaced by the Europeans. The Indian Removal Act of 1830 forced the remaining natives from their lands so that the settlers could build homes for themselves. Over the next eight years almost 100,000 people from the Cherokee were forced to travel to an area referred to as Indian Territory. This area was located in modern day Oklahoma and had a devastating effect on the Cherokee. The natives refer to this forced removal as the Trail of Tears.

The Plains

Stretching from the Mississippi River to the Rocky Mountains from the Gulf of Mexico to modern day Canada, the Plains region was home to smaller cultures who spoke a variety of languages including Uto-Aztecan, Algonquian and Siouan. These people enjoyed a rather stable existence by farming and hunting. When the settlers introduced the use of horses in the 1700s, the native peoples began a nomadic lifestyle in which they would forage and find food by travelling long distances. Some of the well-known groups such as the Comanche, Blackfeet and the Crow chased buffalo over the plains and took shelter within their iconic teepees. The teepees were made from the skin of bison and were easily taken down for travel. These tribes were famous for their richly decorated war headdresses that were made from beautiful feathers.

A number of things brought by the European settlers shaped the future of those who lived on the Plains. The Europeans traded kettles, knives and guns to the point that the peoples of the Plains began to rely upon them. The settlers also brought death in the form of various diseases the natives had never experienced before. Their immune systems could not combat small pox and many natives died as a result. The latter part of the 19th century also saw the near annihilation of buffalo herds by the settlers who hunted them for sport. Since the native peoples could not earn a living and the Europeans controlled the lands, the Plains' People had no choice but to move to the reservations created for them by the government.

The Southwest

The Southwest region was spread out across several states including Texas, Utah, Colorado, New Mexico, Arizona and a strip of Mexico, and peoples known as the Yuma, Yaqui, Zuni and the Hopi populated it. Because of the somewhat fertile landscape, the natives were able to grow crops such as maize. Their homes were referred to as pueblos and were made from stone such that they reached several stories in height, it could even be said that they were somewhat similar to small primitive apartment buildings. Within the heart of these communities, the natives built pit houses called the kivas that were used for political meetings and for ceremonies related to religious rites.

Two of the most famous peoples from the Southwest region were the Apache and the Navajo. Unlike others they preferred a much more nomadic lifestyle and survived by hunting or occasionally looting neighboring communities. The Apache and the Navajo did not establish stable communities and homes like the Yuma, but instead created rounded homes out of bark, mud and other simple materials that were known for always facing east.

Once the Mexican War came to an end – when the Southwest region was incorporated into the United States – the majority of the Native Peoples in the area had been killed. The Spanish missionaries captured and made slaves from the Pueblo, who quickly died from being overworked on vast estates that were created for the Spanish. Those that had survived the war were forced by the government to move to one of the Indian Reserves.

The Great Basin

The Great Basin region is located in between the Sierra Nevada and the Rocky Mountains with the Colorado Plateau in the south. The region consists of a mixture of lakes, salt flats and deserts, here a number of peoples who spoke a dialect of the Uto-Aztecan or the Shoshonean languages lived, including the Ute, Paiute and the Bannock. They survived by hunting animals such as lizards and by eating any plants they could find. Their homes were known as wikiups and were created by using poles made from willow trees; they were not permanent so it was very easy to move them in case of an emergency. Also, they had their own form of government, which involved invocations and input from their leaders.

When the Europeans moved into the area, the peoples in the Great Basin region purchased horses and created hunting parties that would go on to raid neighboring tribes. When, during the middle of the 19th century, the settlers discovered the area was rich in gold and silver, they took over the land while the natives did not want to leave, and so most of them were killed.

California

California was the most populated cultural region because of the great climate and fertile land. Historians estimate that California had around 300,000 people living within its boundaries during the middle of the 16th century. It is believed that around one hundred different peoples lived there and spoke over 200 different dialects, most of which originated from the Uto-Aztecan, Hokan and the Penutian languages. It is generally accepted that more languages were spoken in California than all of Europe at the time.

In spite of the vast number of languages spoken in California all who lived there essentially followed the same way of life. They created family units referred to as tribelets and relationships amongst them, for the most part, were peaceful. The Spanish arrived in the region during the mid-16th century with the vision of creating a civilization. They established a church in 1769 in modern day San Diego while enslaving the Indigenous people as laborers. The slaves suffered a similar fate to that of natives in other regions: they were either killed by disease or by being overworked.

The Northwest Coast

Stretching from Canada's British Columbia to North California and its coastline the Northwest region is abundant in materials and resources with a warm temperature. Most of the food that the natives needed came from the nearby rivers since they lived on fish, whales, salmon and other seafood in order to establish permanent communities instead of a nomadic lifestyle. This is one fact that distinguishes the Northwest peoples from others. Also, the communities here were run by a strict social organization that was more complex than organizations in other regions, here an individual's social status was influenced by the number of and quality of ones' possessions, and close ties to the chief meant a higher status for the individual. Some of the better-known groups who lived in the Northwest region were the Salish, Kwakiutlm, Coos, Chinook and the Haida.

The Plateau

Situated within the Fraser and Columbia River drainage basins, the Plateau region was surrounded by several other cultures. This area would be where the states of Washington, Oregon, Montana and Idaho are situated. The majority of people who lived in this region set up small villages along the riverbanks and other bodies of water to live off of fish, game animals, nuts and berries. In the south, the tribes of Yakama, Walla Walla, Modoc and the Klamath spoke dialects of the Penutian language while in the northern regions the tribes spoke a dialect of the Salishan language. These people included the Spokane, Salish and the Skitswish.

Various Indigenous peoples introduced the horse into the Plateau region during the 18th century, and horses quickly became an important part of their culture. The tribes here expanded their trading networks, improved the economy and became intermediaries between the Plains and Northwest peoples. Lewis and Clark, the famous explorers, arrived in the region in 1805. When they saw lush land ready to be taken they called others to come join them, and come they did, so much so that by the end of the 1800s any remaining natives had been either been killed or moved to reservations set up by the government.

The Early Period of the United States of America

The earliest Europeans who attempted to build permanent settlements in what we now call North America were from Spain. Lucas Vazquez de Ayllon arrived in America in 1526, and setting out to establish the first colony in modern day Carolina he was also the first to bring slaves from Africa, but his attempt to stay proved unsuccessful. Those who did not die from disease or starvation quickly deserted the settlement. It wasn't until 39 years later, when Pedro Menendez de Aviles established a colony in modern day St. Augustine in Florida, that it can be said that Europeans now had a permanent foothold in North America.

Sir Humphrey Gilbert was the first British leader who attempted to create a colony after Queen Elizabeth I gave him the rights to establish a Crown Colony in America in 1578. Five years later Gilbert travelled across the ocean with several ships to land in Newfoundland, whereupon he explored the region. After some time they returned home to tell everybody of what they had seen, but Gilbert vanished upon arrival. It was Walter Raleigh, Gilbert's half-brother, who made the next attempt at colonization. He set out with two ships to scout the coastline in 1584 and discovered what was later named Virginia after the Virgin Queen herself. In 1585 Richard Grenville led an expedition with his fellow English crewmen and arrived in July of that year. He left some of his crew on Roanoke Island so that he could return home for more supplies but the colonists deserted the new site due to a shortage of supplies and returned back home.

John White was the next person to try and establish a new colony in America. Women, men and children followed him over to Virginia but, as with Grenville, White was forced to return back to England to gather more supplies. Upon return, he saw that England was at war with Spain and his journey back to America was effectively delayed until 1590. When he arrived in America again, he saw that the colonists had abandoned the site and were nowhere to be found. It is still uncertain as to what exactly happened to these settlers.

Jamestown and Virginia

Others from England tried to colonize America but failed due to a lack of resources and it wasn't until 1606, when the Virginia Company first sent out expeditions, that anyone actually succeeded. The Company sent two expeditions including one that was led by Raleigh Gilbert, the son of Sir Humphrey Gilbert. They arrived in modern day Maine in 1606 but abandoned the colony three years later. In 1607, the second voyage arrived in what was known as Jamestown.

Two years later another wave of settlers arrived in Jamestown but they – like the settlers before – them experienced many hardships too. There was disease, starvation and war with the natives, all of these events resulted in the death of many settlers. By the following year those who had survived were ready to abandon the colony, and it was only on the arrival of a new wave of settlers from England that they agreed to stay. Sir Thomas Dale arrived the year after and while he was Governor, he enacted strict laws to keep everyone safe in the community. Anyone who broke those laws faced severe consequences many times in the form of harsh penalties.

John Rolfe is famous for growing tobacco since, after two years of hard toil, he sold tobacco back in England and was able to improve the colony's economy. The Virginia Company gave those who wanted to cross the ocean a choice, they could either fund their own journey and be receive 50 acres of land upon arrival, or, if unable to afford to do that, work for the Virginia Company as servants.

The Virginia Company was disbanded in 1624 when the English Crown took control of the colony while it had a population of around 27,000. Within 50 years the population had grown to 78,000, which of course presented the people with the accompanying problems of such a large number of inhabitants, for instance the mosquitos in Jamestown caused malaria, and the main government building had burned down several times. In 1699, in an attempt to resolve these issues, the local government center was officially transferred to Middle Plantation, where, over time, the governor renamed the settlement as Williamsburg, a place that still exists today.

The Pilgrim Fathers

1620 saw the establishment of an additional colony by the English, but these settlers had come to the New World to escape religious persecution, because they opposed the teachings of the Church of England. They wished to settle in a place where they could practice their own religious beliefs and are known today as the Pilgrim Fathers. They embarked on their journey across the Atlantic Ocean on the *Mayflower* and eventually made the shores of North America in December 1620. Around 50% of those who arrived died within a year and those who survived learned from the natives how to grow crops in a land so different to their own. In 1628, another settlement was created in Salem.

With the founding of the Massachusetts Bay Company in 1649 the following years saw the arrival of even more Europeans, which once again significantly increased the population. Many other new towns were being created at this time, including Wethersfield town that was established in 1634 in Connecticut. Two years later a group of settlers abandoned Massachusetts Bay and established the town of Providence on Rhode Island.

Most of the states in the South had an agricultural economy. However, the New England colonies were based on commerce and depended heavily on the fishing industry. The settlers traded fish, timber and furs to further grow the regional economy.

As the colonists' population grew the Europeans and Indigenous peoples repeatedly found themselves in bloody conflicts with each other. The Pequot tribe was wiped out during the Pequot War between 1634 and 1638, while King

Philip's War broke out in 1675 between the natives and the settlers; it is rather ironic that King Philip was actually a native named Metacom. The war came to an end in 1678 after Metacom was killed while running away from the English and a final treaty known as the Treaty of Casco Bay was signed by the natives to prevent another war, both sides had suffered great losses, but in the end the natives were far outnumbered by the Europeans.

Battles with Britain

The American colonies began to have a strained relationship with Britain and frustration grew as time passed. For the British the colonies were established to assist the homeland, but the Colonies had their own interests to protect. In 1651 a new law was passed that prohibited them from trading with the Netherlands, France, Spain and their respective colonies. The idea was to restrict American trade so only Britain would benefit from her riches. This began a series of acts known as the Navigation Acts.

The population of the colonies in North America kept on growing during the 18th century with historians estimating it to have been around 300,000 by the latter part of the 17th century but more than a million in 1760. Over the next two decades the population doubled and caused settlers to expand their territories. Finally, immigrants from Northern Ireland, Scotland, Germany and other countries began arriving in the colonies in search of a new life.

The Great Proclamation

The relationship between the mother country and the new colonies continued to decline after the mid-18th century. Canada was now in the hands of the British but it had been an expensive endeavor, also, in 1763, the British issued the Great

Proclamation that caused total uproar as it stated that the colonists could not settle anywhere further than the start of the rivers that ended in the Atlantic Ocean. This announcement was ignored and tensions continued to grow because the colonists wished to create settlements in different parts of the land.

The next year saw the passing of the Sugar Act that is officially known as the American Revenue Act. At the time the colonists were not paying as much taxes as the British citizens and the British government wished to change the agreement. The Act forced the colonists to pay higher taxes on molasses and thus the colonists' resentment deepened even more.

It was the Stamp Act issued in 1765 that finally saw the slogan *No Taxation Without Representation* spring to life. The British began taxing newspapers and cards, which greatly angered the colonists so they retaliated by boycotting goods from Britain and stopped paying debts to British traders. When the British saw what had happened, they repealed the Stamp Act the following year and issued the Declaratory Act that clearly stated that the British government ruled the colonies in America.

Two years later Charles Townshend began taxing tea, oil, paints and other goods. The colonists again began a boycott of goods and Britain was forced to repeal the taxes, and so it was that by 1770 the British government received taxes only from tea, because all other types of goods had become exempt from taxation.

Trouble in Boston and the Boston Tea Party

In March 1770 a group of British soldiers found themselves being hit with snowballs thrown by some colonists. The

British soldiers, instead of dealing with the situation maturely, killed five and wounded another six with gunfire. Six out of the eight soldiers were acquitted of the crimes while the other two were punished for manslaughter, which meant that their thumbs were branded. The colonists were outraged at the British for not executing those that they deemed to have murdered their fellow colonists.

Three years later the British East India Company arrived in Boston to sell 298 boxes of tea. At the time Boston hated the British and so a number of Americans disguised themselves as natives and dumped the tea into the water. This would later come to be known as the Boston Tea Party. The Prime Minister at the time was Lord North who imposed a succession of new laws known as the Intolerable Acts, Boston's port was also shut down and the administration center was transferred to Salem.

More resentment ensued when the British attempted to gain the loyalty of the French Catholics through the Quebec Act in 1774 by effectively allowing the borders to expand to the south and west of Quebec, now believing that the British wanted to relocate the French Catholics in the region to gain more power, the Continental Congress arranged a meeting. They wished for both of the previous Acts to be repealed so colonists, identifying with an ever-growing sense of being American, could assert their own laws and taxes.

In the same year Joseph Galloway attempted to make a compromise, suggesting that the American colonies should create a Grand Council and let the Crown select a President General. The Continental Congress voted for the idea but the British refused to compromise with the colonists. In February of 1775 the British government declared Massachusetts to be in rebellion, and sent British forces to handle the situation and quickly shut any thoughts of revolt.

The American colonists resisted by forming their own militia and in April of the same year, the British tried to take control of an American arms supply close to Concord but the Americans had been forewarned about British intentions. The Americans faced the British in a battle and eight Americans were killed; however, the arms supply had already been removed from the area so the British did not obtain what they had come looking for and were forced to withdraw back to Boston. With over seventy British soldiers dead and either 200 dead or missing, it was the beginning of the American Revolutionary War.

Until March of the following year the British, under siege, were forced to stay in Boston and could only receive supplies via sea through the British navy. However, despite the extra supplies, the British had limited resources and only some knowledge of the surrounding area. In May reinforcements from Britain arrived in Boston to help lift the siege but to no avail, so as a last resort the British withdrew to Canada by using the ships they had at their disposal.

In May 1775 Congress assembled for another critical meeting where they discussed the need for a military that would protect America for centuries to come. The Commander in Chief was George Washington who tried to compromise with the British but King George III declined. In August of the same year the king declared all colonies as rebel colonies and stated that they would be dealt with according to British Law, the Continental Congress ignored the decree and agreed that the American people needed their own government. As a result, the American colonies created their own state constitutions, which effectively replaced Crown Laws.

Common Sense by Tom Paine was published the next year, with the author suggesting that Congress should not need to negotiate with Britain for anything. The book quickly became popular among the public for its independence ideas.

On June 7th 1776 the Continental Congress was issued a document by Richard Henry Lee that stated America should be completely independent and that Congress should forge relationships with other countries to fight Britain. Four days later, Congress selected a group to pen the Declaration of Independence that was signed on the fourth of July.

The American Revolution

When the American Revolution began the British certainly had a larger army and more resources at their disposal but a huge disadvantage that couldn't overcome was the length of delay in communications. Ships generally took around seven weeks to sail from London to America and messages had to be sent via letters because there were no certainly no phones or telecommunication devices available at the time.

Britain initially won some major battles in 1776, notably at Long Island and New York that resulted in Washington's withdrawal. The Americans, however, won victories at Trenton and then Princeton. The British won at Brandywine in 1777 but Washington won at Saratoga the same year. British forces made their way down from Canada but were trapped by the Americans and had no choice but to withdraw.

The French believed that the British would lose the war and seized this opportunity to join the war against their long-time enemy. In 1778 France joined America in its fight against Britain and caused the British great difficulties in resupplying their army in America. The Spanish and the Dutch joined the fight in the next two years by allying themselves with the Americans. Britain was overwhelmed by so many nations fighting against it and was forced to keep the majority of its army within European territory to protect the homeland.

Washington gained victories at Kings Mountain and then at Cowpens in 1780-1781. The British were under the leadership of Cornwallis who made the wrong decision to concentrate at Yorktown in Virginia where his army became trapped on all sides: the French navy blocked the ocean and the Americans had lined up on land. Having no choice the British surrendered and suffered a great loss. Although they had lost the war, the Revolutionary War carried on for another two years before it was officially ended in 1783 on the signing of the Treaty of Paris.

The Foundation of the United States of America

The states had been originally grouped together in a somewhat loose confederation in 1777, but all of the states sent representatives to a meeting in Philadelphia to create a more formal arrangement. A new constitution was drafted in 1787 and two years later, George Washington was elected as the First President of the United States of America. In 1791 the Bill of Rights was created with the famous first ten amendments.

The population of the United States continued to grow at a rapid pace during the 18th and 19th centuries. From all over Europe new migrants came and settled in America while the existing Americans began to migrate to the west and found new cities as they settled down. Vermont became the 14th state in 1791, Kentucky was founded the following year and Tennessee was also added to the ever-growing list of American states in 1796. At the turn of the 19th century America purchased Louisiana from France but with great economic strain. The French lands came at an expensive price of $15,000,000 – remember this is in 1812 – but ultimately came to be admitted as the 18th State of the Union.

The 1812 War

At the time of the Louisiana Purchase, as it is now known, America and Britain were locked in yet another conflict. The British had blocked Atlantic ports against Napoleon, thus preventing the Americans from carrying out commerce by way of the ocean. To add to the rising tension British forces arrested deserters on Americans ships, some of who were not considered to be as such by the Americans. Furthermore, America was eyeing the region to the north and wished to invade Canada. The Congress officially supported the invasion, but not everyone in the public realm was so eager to launch yet another war. It was ultimately a divided country that led to the failure of the incursion.

With Napoleon's abdication in 1814 the British were now able to send more troops to America, they captured Washington in the same year, even setting fire to the White House after ransacking it for valuables. However, they were forced to retreat within a couple of weeks and a peace treaty was drawn up which was to be signed later that year.

The Advancement of America

By the turn of the 19th century it is estimated that the population had grown to more than 7 million people. It reached more than 9 million in 1820 and then rose to

17,000,000 after 20 years. America was adding more states to expand its territory, the most notable state being Indiana, added in 1816.

The American economy began to develop quickly with the production of cotton in the southern states. On the other side of the Atlantic, Britain was experiencing a massive surge in the cotton industry and ended up purchasing vast amounts of the raw material from America. Over half of the cotton in the world was produced within USA by the mid-19th century while the coal mining industry became very prevalent during the early 19th century.

Infrastructure was being built to support the ever-growing population including bridges, roads, homes and offices that gained serious traction during this time. A canal was commissioned from the Hudson River all the way to Lake Erie in 1817 and was finally finished in 1825. This canal resulted in a massive reduction in the costs of transporting goods from one location to another. After a few years, the country's first railways were built in New Jersey and Massachusetts.

In 1814 the Indigenous peoples from Florida and the Americans in Georgia began experiencing new problems, tribes were allowing slaves who had run away from their masters to hide amongst them, which the Americans did not like. The Seminole War began in 1821 when Andrew Jackson led American forces into Florida to fight the Spanish. In 1821 the Americans took Florida from Spain and it became a new American state.

The American Civil War

The American Civil War occurred from 1861 to 1865 and is the bloodiest conflict in American history, occurring between what were known as the Union and the Confederate States. The Unionists included 23 free states and 5 border states, all of which were led by Abraham Lincoln. Those in opposition, the Confederate States, were all located within the Southern USA and refused the new policy changes initiated by the national government. There was a significantly different view of political structure, social structure and the legal status of slavery between the two sides. Abraham Lincoln and his supporters wished to ban slavery but the Confederate States saw this as an attempt to curtail their rights, since they held the view that each state should have a right to create specific laws concerning its own social structure.

One of the earliest battles recorded begins with General Beauregard from the Confederate States, where on taking command of around 22,000 soldiers in 1861 at the Manassas Junction, he was attacked by General McDowell and 30,000 Union troops. McDowell seemed to have the upper hand at first but was forced to retreat when Thomas Jackson brought reinforcements from the south.

In April of 1862 the Unionists were able to secure an important victory at Shiloh and although the Confederates won some important battles, they were incapable of driving the Unionists back entirely. Fresh troops arrived that same night to aid the Unionists, which resulted in the Confederates having to withdraw. New Orleans fell under the control of the Unionists first and then too came Baton Rouge the following month.

That same year General McClellan commenced the Peninsular Campaign and was able to take control of Yorktown in May and by the end of the month he finally made it to Richmond. In June, General Robert E. Lee attacked during the Seven

Days battles and McClellan had no choice but to withdraw. During late summer, Generals McClellan and Lee faced each other at the Second Manassas where the South won and the North was force into retreat. General Lee started marching towards the north and once again met McClellan on the battlefield at Antietam, but this time it was the Confederate army that was forced to retreat.

On December 13, 1862, the Confederates secured a great victory over the Unionists at Fredericksburg and then again at Chancellorsville the following May. In the early summer of 1863 General Lee marched back to the north in preparation for the Battle of Gettysburg, which was the most decisive battle of the entire American Civil War. Between the first and third of July the two armies fought each other viciously. Initially the Confederates had the upper hand but they suffered heavy losses and had no choice but to leave the filed of battle and when they lost at Vicksburg, General Grant was there to seize every quarter and it was from this point onwards that the Confederate forces began to decline. They made another push at Chattanooga to try and change the course of the war in November of the same year but were again defeated by the Unionists.

General Sherman marched down to Georgia, arrived in Atlanta – massively important to the Union's logistics and supplies – in 1864 and captured Savannah before marching towards South Carolina. He was able to take control of Columbia in 1865 before pressing towards North Carolina.

The war came to an end when the Union's General Grant's men finally overran General Lee. Initially he had evacuated his forces from Richmond – the Confederate's capital – and Petersburg in April 1864, but when he saw there was no chance of winning, he surrendered to General Grant and ended the war. The remaining Confederate forces also surrendered to the Unionists by the end of May 1864. Regrettably President Lincoln did not live to see the conclusion of the war and the ensuing peace, because John Wilkes Booth assassinated him in April of that year at Ford's Theatre.

Slavery

Slavery was carried to the American Colonies when African slaves were brought to Jamestown, Virginia in 1619, the purpose being to use their labor to facilitate crop production, notably cotton. In only a few years African slaves could be found most anywhere throughout the colonies. The invention of the cotton gin further increased the need for their sweat and toil, and sweat and toil they did. It was off the back of their labor that a new economic foundation for America was built.

Slavery began in America while the British were still in control and it continued after the American Revolution. Slavery was initially a way of replacing expensive labor with a cheaper form of work as African slaves worked in tobacco, rice and indigo production. Slavery soon became a necessity in America and it tempted every person who owned a small piece of land to attain slaves so that work could be done cheaply. Slavery did face some opposition from the government but it was mostly the northern states that raised their voice against the practice, they being 'Free States'. It did not sway the South who continued to exploit this human resource at a terrible cost. The South's economy soon became dependent on slaves to such an extent that they were willing to go to war if any were to threaten its practice.

Many viewed slavery as a similar form of oppression to that which the Americans had faced when the British forced their laws upon the colonists. The American Revolution did not deliver as radical a change to the law as many people thought it would and the Constitution did not provide equal rights to Africans who were considered to be lower in status than Caucasian people.

It is well known that slavery was a brutal, abhorrent practice and many supported the abolition movement that was aimed at removing all forms of slavery via the Constitution. The abolition movement rose to prominence and was led by many free black men such as Fredrick Douglass and others. There were of course also white supporters of the abolition movement. The media extensively covered the topic of slavery and many editorials spoke about slavery as a sin, and there were others who detailed how ineffective slavery was in the development of the economy, and that America should use more efficient ways to produce cotton.

Eventually many slaves started escaping with the help of their supporters who set up the Underground Railroad. Thousands of slaves escaped to the north since it was also known as the free land. Harriet Tubman is known for her role in helping slaves escape to Canada and is a great figure in American history, she helped to establish tunnels that could be used to escape, even making the journey several times with different families so that they could have a better life.

The End of the Slave Trade

During the American Civil War the Unionists and the Confederates were fighting for many reasons, one of which was the right to abolish slavery. President Lincoln was somewhat hesitant in abolishing slavery initially but eventually changed his views, and with that change of mind the Emancipation Proclamation was declared on the 23rdof September 1862, an act which granted freedom to slaves in the rebel states at the beginning of 1863. This was quickly amended through the 13th amendment and freedom was granted to all slaves.

The Union won the civil war and it led to legislative repealing of slavery but that did not mean that the struggle for black people was over. The 13th amendment abolished slavery and the constitution was officially amended, which meant that African Americans were now legally equal to Caucasians, but the new laws were violated and at times ignored, in many instances on both a local and state level.

The fight against racial discrimination continued for the next 100 years as African Americans faced inequality in various forms. Former slaves had difficulty finding work and many were forced to live in poverty, and the new laws led to the rise of hate groups such as the Ku Klux Klan, which propagated hate speech and divisions. So much so that they unleashed a horrendous brutally that saw African Americans lynched, murdered and beaten simply for not being white.

Furthermore, governments at the state and local levels enacted the Jim Crow laws; these laws "recognised" black people as being equal to whites but required both groups to remain separate from each other. The public infrastructure was divided so as they did not share the same space as white people.

Finally, the Civil Rights Movement struggle for social justice – which mainly took place during the 1950s and 1960s – successfully launched various protests and boycotts to bring about an end to white hegemony. The struggle was difficult and time-consuming and many people died. Notable people who led the struggle to freedom included Martin Luther King Jr., Malcolm X, Rosa Parks and Thurgood Marshall, it was on the back of this movement that Jim Crow laws were finally repealed.

As time passed new laws were introduced to help African Americans with jobs and other needs and there is now a severe penalty for racially segregating or discriminating against not just the black, but any community.

Montgomery Bus Boycott

Rosa Parks is best known for the famous Montgomery Bus Boycott where she held true to her beliefs and did not give her seat to a standing white person. The prevailing laws and customs at that time dictated that bus passengers should be segregated on the basis of their race. The front seats of every bus were reserved for white people, with blacks were required to sit at the back. It was also thought to be a normal practice for black people to give their seat to white people when any were standing.

On December 1, 1955, after a tiring day at work, Mrs. Parks boarded the Cleveland Avenue Bus, paid her fare and sat in the 'colored' section beginning from the middle of the bus. Her seat was directly behind the seats reserved for whites and ironically the driver was the same person who had refused to allow Mrs. Parks to enter the bus from the front in 1943.

The bus ran its normal route and the 'white only' seats in front of Rosa began to fill up, as more white passengers entered the bus it got to the point where there was no room to sit and many were standing. The driver then asked the black passengers including Mrs. Parks to give up their seats to the white passengers who were standing. Three of the four black people who were also sitting at the time did so, not Mrs. Parks. She refused.

The driver threatened Mrs. Parks and stated that he would call the police if she did not move from her seat but she remained resolute. She did not move and declared that the driver could call the police if he wished to do so. Her act of defiance became a fight for rights she deserved, which later became recorded in history. She was arrested by a police officer for "breaking the law" to which Rosa Parks replied that she was being arrested because "white people like to push black people around".

Edgar Nixon, who was the president of the Montgomery chapter of the NAACP, bailed Rosa out of jail the next day. Her protest became popular among Americans and encouraged others to fight for their rights since there was a strong push to abandon sectional seating on the basis of race. Mrs. Parks also challenged her arrest in court and addressed the legality of racial segregation. Rosa Parks' arrest put pressure on the Supreme Court, which finally ruled that racial segregation was illegal and unconstitutional. This later became known as the historical case of Browder v. Gayle.

March on Washington

Martin Luther King Jr. was born on January 15, 1929 in Atlanta, Georgia. He had two siblings, an older sister and a younger brother. Growing up King Jr. often saw his father take part in protests against segregation that was enforced by the government. He is also known to have befriended a white boy when he was young, a friend that would go to a different school for whites only, while he would go to a school for blacks. Later this friendship would be forced to an end because the father of the white boy did not want him to play with Martin.

King was the representative of the SCLC and organized a march on Washington as part of the Civil Rights Movement. The march aimed to secure jobs and freedom for the African American community, a cause that was also supported by President John F. Kennedy, since he wished to make legislative changes to ensure the end of racial segregation.

The actual goal of the march had been to denounce the government for not safeguarding the rights of the African American community. It was supposed to vividly demonstrate the harsh conditions black people were living in and the daily inequality they faced, but instead it took a more moderate tone because of the president's influence and as a result many civil rights groups denounced King, seeing the march as a farce.

The march was full of tensions and doubts about its success, but many still took the opportunity to join it anyway. It was a call to end racial discrimination and racial injustice, to provide a fixed minimum wage, to create job opportunities and to form a government that included both white and black people. There were approximately 250,000 people who attended the march and the crowds filled the lawns of the Lincoln memorial all the way to the National Mall, such was the attendance that it was the largest gathering of protesters in the history of Washington at the time.

Martin Luther King Jr. addressed the crowd with his famous "I have a dream" speech, a speech that inspired with its soaring rhetoric and message of reconciliation and hope and it helped cement King as a colossus of modern American history. On October 14, 1964, King was awarded the Nobel Peace Prize for his work in the Civil Rights Movement.

Chapter 5– Australian History

The Aborigines of Australia are considered to be the world's oldest continuous people, since it is generally accepted that their ancestors arrived in Australia a minimum of 50,000 years ago via boats. When the Europeans arrived there was an estimated 1,000,000 Aborigines living throughout the country as hunter-gatherers. There were 500 tribes or nations present across the country and they spoke around 700 languages at the time, known for traveling large distances to trade and to conduct ceremonies their landscape included lush rainforests, snowy mountains and vast deserts.

The Aboriginal Nations believed in The Dreaming, which is also known as Tjukurrpa. Ancient Aborigine mythology tells how The Great Spirit Ancestors created all life and land and that these spirits also connected everything in the past and present through signs. The Dreaming myths of the spirit ancestors were retold through different mediums such as stories, art, dancing and singing.

Britain's Colonization of Australia

The Aborigines lived without interference from outsiders until the 17th century when the first European ships landed on the Australian coastline. When Captain James Cook arrived in 1770, the British colonized the country along its eastern coast. The initially colonies were founded to house convicts, because British prisons were overcrowded. On January 26, 1788, a fleet of 11 ships known as the First Fleet arrived in Australia carrying 1,500 people; approximately half of these people were criminals who had been convicted by the British government. In 1868 the last penal ship arrived in Australia, a practice that saw an estimated 160,000 convicted men and women transported in this manner.

At the end of the 18th century free settlers began to arrive in Australia but found life was more difficult than what they had imagined. Men who committed crimes were hanged or severely flogged for minor offences such as stealing, and women were frequently raped and abused since there were five times as many men compared to the number of women.

It was not just the European settlers who found themselves under threat because these newcomers, or "invaders" brought illnesses and death to the Aboriginal Nations through a variety of diseases that they had no resistance to, also a lot of peoples lost their land and their lifestyle was changed forever.

Squatters Migrate Across Australia

In the early 19th century freed convicts, soldiers and others transformed the barren land given to them by the government into thriving farms. The British people heard about the great prospects to be had in Australia, which resulted in more ships sailing out from Britain. Known as squatters, these people made their way deeper into the lands of the Aborigines while looking for land of their own and fresh water for their livestock.

White settlement in Australia was relatively small in the first three decades after the arrival of the First Fleet, mainly because the Napoleonic Wars had delayed transportation. By 1810 the white population of New South Wales had increased to 12,000 and was mostly made up of convicts and military personnel with a few lawyers, clergymen and doctors. Over the next seven decades, Australia's non-Indigenous population increased substantially to reach 406,000 by 1850, but on the eve of the gold rush the population rose dramatically to 1,648,000 by 1870. The next three decades witnessed further demographic growth with a huge surge in immigration until the population reached 3,770,000 at the time of the Federation on January 1st 1901, when Australia officially became a nation. By then some 78% of Australians had been born in Australia, 18% in the British Isles, 2% in other European countries and less than 2% in Asian or Pacific countries.

Between 1831 and 1900 around half of the 1.47 million migrants to Australia had passages subsidized by the British government. They were recruited under the systematic colonization policies of Edward Gibbon Wakefield, whereby revenue from Australian sales was used to subsidize passages on government-sponsored ships. However, other schemes also existed whereby immigrants were selected and recruited. The great majority of settlers in Australia came from British or Irish backgrounds and it is helpful to refer to them as Anglo-Celtic because Britain and the whole of Ireland were politically joined at the time (Until the declaration of the Irish Free State in 1921). There were notable differences between the British and Irish immigrants in their religious allegiances because most Irish immigrants were Catholic, many English settlers were Anglican and many Scots were Presbyterian. Since all of these groups held widely diverse views about education, culture, and politics, it can be said that 19th-century Australia was multicultural, but only within an Anglo-Celtic context.

Colonists partly came from middle-class professional backgrounds, but predominantly from lower-class skilled and semi-skilled occupations. Few aristocrats immigrated to Australia because they had no need to seek out opportunities in such a faraway destination, the social structure of colonial Australia was therefore heavily biased towards the bottom part of a vertical pyramid that denoted social class. Apart from the predominant British and Irish contingent, other smaller groups were also found in the region. German Lutherans helped to settle parts of South Australia in the 1830s and 1840s while Chinese migrants were found in the gold rush settlements. Polynesians, Melanesians, and a few Italians found work in the sugar-producing tropical zone of Queensland. All of these migrants retained their ethnic identities while adapting to life in Australia. Before the 1880s, the colonists thought of themselves as Queenslanders, Victorians, South Australians, and so on, but as time passed, these groups began to view themselves as Australians with the rise of a homogeneous community.

The growth of white settlement in Australia stemmed from various factors, with one of them being the spread of pioneers or ex-convicts children beyond the Blue Mountains. They continued overland and made homes in fertile bush areas that were suitable for sheep grazing in the interior of New South Wales and the Port Phillip District. Australia Felix, the name used by Thomas Mitchell for lush pastures in western Victoria, was also a popular destination for settlement. By 1803 settlers from New South Wales had migrated to Van Diemen's Land, which became a colony in 1824. New colonies were established in Western Australia including the Swan River colony (1829), South Australia (1836), Victoria (1850), and Queensland (1859). At this time, Victoria still had the post-1843 boundaries of the Port Phillip District since South Australia, Victoria and Queensland were carved out of a 'greater' New South Wales. Eventually, in 1856, Van Diemen's Land was renamed Tasmania.

Each colony established a capital city and port: Sydney in New South Wales, Hobart in Van Diemen's Land, Perth and Fremantle in Western Australia, Adelaide and Port Adelaide in

South Australia, Melbourne in Victoria, and Brisbane in Queensland. These colonial capitals absorbed most of the settlers because they were connected to productive hinterlands with the exception of Perth. Population growth and the spread of settlement were also stimulated by economic opportunities in urban trades, pastoral occupations, and mineral excavation.

It is common knowledge that settlers competed with Aborigines for control over land and resources, and although completely different in nature these cultural groups often cooperated with each other, however, there were many examples of friction and violence. Clashes occurred between Aborigines and settlers in the Hawkesbury River area of New South Wales in the 1790s in a serious incident that is recorded and often mentioned in history. Settlers fired upon Indigenous people claiming they had damaged their crops and the Aborigines retaliated by forming their own raiding parties. Between 1824 and 1836 settlers persuaded Governor George Arthur in Van Diemen's Land that the Aborigines were a treacherous race, so as a result he pursued a draconian policy of driving Indigenous people away from settled areas to the western fringes of the island. In 1838 the Liverpool plains area of what is now northern New South Wales experienced a series of massacres of Indigenous people. On June 10, a massacre occurred at Myall Creek station where settlers killed 30 unarmed Aborigines as revenge for attacks on their livestock.

While Aborigines suffered from colonial expansion, settlers generally flourished. By the second half of the 19th century Australia had acquired a reputation as a working man's paradise since most people had a better living standard than those in a similar position in Britain. Australians enjoyed

124

greater meat consumption than the British and on average earned higher wages. They often had better housing stock mainly due to the fact that it was newer; furthermore, workplace arrangements were protected by stronger trade unions than in Britain. By the 1880s Sydney's Manly – a suburb on its north shore – epitomized the working person's position in the southern hemisphere. As the slogan put it, it was 'Seven miles from Sydney and a thousand miles from care'.

This rosy picture is not the whole story, because colonial Australia was more of a working man's paradise for skilled people rather than for the unskilled. Economic booms and busts affected employment opportunities, especially in the agricultural slump of the early 1840s and the economic depression in the early 1890s. The highly seasonal nature of the Australian colonial workforce had important implications for working life, such as uneven earnings across one year for many workers. Moreover, there were always Australians who were out of luck and dependent on charity. Poor sanitary conditions in late 19th-century slums in Sydney and Melbourne also affected the image of Australia as a destination for the working class.

Gold, Migrants, and Rebellions

Around 1851 the European settlers began to discover gold, a discovery that soon attracted the attention of China as well as other countries around the globe.

Back in the state of Victoria, the British government had imposed a license on those mining gold, which caused bloody rebellions in 1854 that are referred to as the Eureka Stockade. The government was victorious over the miners but they did gain something as they were given additional rights –

including the vote – and the ability to stand for parliament as long as they possessed a license. It is from this point onwards that Australia is seen to be evolving into a democracy.

Growth and Economy

The Aborigines had cultivated land and food for over 50,000 years before the Europeans arrived. The Europeanization of Australia involved exploration of the interior for minerals to help Australia establish better international relations through shipping, trade, and migration. Unexpected factors helped to shape a distinctive Australian continental experience, such as the sudden discovery of gold in the early 1850s and the subsequent rush of people to the goldfields in search of their fortunes. Land availability, assisted migration, and the rise of a skilled workforce led to the growth of an expanding pastoral frontier in which bush life became embedded in the Australian psyche.

Urbanization also became a prime element of the Australian experience as colonial capital cities became magnets for immigrants. The growth of seaport cities as intermediaries for the exchange of Australia's raw materials established strong and lasting connections between Australia and the wider world. There was often a conflict of interest between the need for extracting natural resources versus preserving the flora and fauna of the land. While these changes occurred, Indigenous people struggled to cope with an ever-changing landscape.

The Aborigines had survived for tens of millennia in Australia through a distinctive approach to gathering food and by utilizing a spiritual connection they had developed with the land. They had intimate knowledge of particular territories associated with their tribal beliefs; the rocks, bushes, rivers, flora, and fauna of the landscape were the spiritual home of their ancestors and deserved respect. The Aborigines had no desire for individual acquisitiveness in their material life: all food and artifacts were shared among the group in a spirit of mutuality that satisfied communal needs. Sharing provided mutual help in times of scarcity and they saw no need to acquire land through entrepreneurial practices. Furthermore, they had no legal procedures or the expansionist mentality of the foreign settlers, in fact there were relatively few instances of Aborigines raiding the territorial lands of other tribes as identity with the land was both an intellectual and economic feature of Aboriginal life. Indigenous people connected their whole beings to the prophecies of the 'Dreaming' stories, which explained how they should conduct themselves.

The Aborigines adjusted to climate change by monitoring the habitats of plants, game animals and water holes and they developed and improved various tools such as the digging stick, spatula, fishing nets, boomerangs, 'woomera', hammers and spears. Their hunter-gatherer lifestyle did not remain static but altered according to new ecological and climate changes. Yet, as times changed, as changes were forced upon them, they became essential to the sheep farmers of both Western Australia and central Queensland and by 1900 there were around 10,000 Aborigines working for the Europeans.

The Birth of a Nation

On January 1, 1901, Australia became a nation with six states and a single constitution. Today the country is home to people who have immigrated from over 200 different countries. There are over 300 languages spoken and many ethnicities to be found in different parts of the country.

Australia and Wars

World War I broke out and caused destruction throughout Australian society during the early 20th century. By 1914 Australia had a population of about 3,000,000 men of which 420,000 volunteered to fight. Historians estimate that 60,000 men died and several thousand were wounded in the war. After the war, the government initiated the Soldier Settler Scheme, which awarded compensation and farmland to war veterans.

With the Roaring Twenties, the importing of cars, music and movies, the Australian community began to love anything that was British in origin. At the end of the 1920s the Great Depression occurred causing numerous financial organizations to collapse and the gap between the wealthy and the poor to become wider, it was now people turned to sports, such as sailing and cricket, to forget the negativity the country was experiencing.

The Arrival of New Australians

With the onset of World War II Australian women discovered that there were new job positions they could fill while the men were away fighting. The workforce changed once again when countless migrants from all around the world – including the Middle East and the European continent – arrived with the war's end in 1945, the majority of these people found positions in the increasingly prosperous manufacturing industry.

Through the 1950s the Australian economy thrived with great construction projects such as the famous Sydney Opera House and the Snow Mountains Hydroelectric Scheme, the country also became abundant in various natural resources such as timber, wheat and metals. Life was good, and by the end of the 1960s over 70% of the population owned their own homes.

The Relaxation of Australia

At the start of the 1960s, Australia, as many Western countries, experienced the counterculture phenomenon. Australia also had a vast number of ethnic groups and saw a shift in social attitudes, as well as various political changes. In 1967 a vote was cast to determine as whether voting rights would be given to the Aborigines as citizens of the country. A majority voted yes and new laws were created in favor of the Aborigines, but because there was opposition to some of these new policies, there were protests carried out by both Australians and the Aborigines.

Led by Gough Whitlam the Australian Labor Party was voted to power in 1972, which meant that the Liberal and Country Party had to step down. The new party scrapped National Service (peace time conscription) and established free health care within three years. Australian policies that negatively impacted the Aborigines were repealed to pave a new way forward. Furthermore, university was made free, women were given the same salaries as men, ethnic diversity was welcomed and no-fault divorces were granted to the people.

Despite these great reforms the Governor General toppled the new government by exposing it for being corrupt. When the next general election came around the Labor Party was utterly defeated and replaced by the Liberal-National Coalition until the mid-1980s.

Australia and the Sea

The Australian National Anthem declares that 'our home is girt by sea,' which means 'our home is surrounded by sea', a reminder about the life that lives in the sea. In the centuries before European settlement northern Australia had maritime connections with the Macassan trepang fishery for the Chinese market. Also, boats from Java and other parts of Indonesia occasionally touched Australian shores to trade with the Aborigines, and while the Aboriginal population mainly concentrated on land resources they did use small craft for fishing and/or local transport. Australia's maritime development came gradually with European settlement, with its beginnings able to be traced back to 1788 with the settling of a convict colony at Port Jackson, since then Australian life has been significantly influenced by the interaction between its people and the sea.

The modern Australian economy has been shaped by having access to ports, the growth of shipping and ship owning, the progress of coastal, regional and overseas trade, the development of merchant firms, and links between the major port gateways and their hinterlands. This has also caused the emergence of a strong maritime workforce in the Southern Hemisphere.

The growth of tourism, beach culture, ferries and harbor services in and around major conurbations has also led to the development of modern Australian social history. Each Australian state capital is located either on or near a port that provides easy access to the ocean and connections with productive hinterlands. This reflects the early European settlements of Australia, which were initially based within easy reach of the coast.

Sydney and Hobart, both with fine natural harbors, had become flourishing centers for shipping and trade by the early 19th century. In both cases wharves and quays were the site of the first houses in each city and the pattern of housing stretched inland from these initial sites.

Adelaide and Melbourne were founded on the Torrens and Yarra rivers, respectively and after some time ports were eventually built at Port Adelaide and Port Melbourne, while Williamstown also served as a port for Melbourne and Brisbane had a riverside setting. Perth, on the Swan River, had no suitable harbor for vessels because of the shallow estuary on which it was situated, so instead Fremantle was built at the river's mouth to service Perth and its accompanying hinterland.

Each of these cities established shipping facilities and gradually became linked through coastal and regional trade. Overseas liners worked around the coast to discharge the goods they brought and took on cargo for the return voyage. The Australasian Steam Navigation Company was one of the national companies that played a leading role in the development of coastal trade between the 1850s and 1880s when ships sailed from Rockhampton in Queensland to Albany in Western Australia.

Britain dominated long-distance shipping to Australia in the 19th century due to the relaxation of the British East India Company's charter in 1813, which gave its vessels more incentive to come to Australia because of freight commerce. Passengers became equally as important because convicts had to be sent on naval vessels to New South Wales before 1840. After this free transit emigrants began to use government-assisted passages for travel.

British-owned vessels dominated the steam services between Europe and Australia, which began regularly in 1852. The SS Great Britain, Isambard Kingdom Brunel's passenger ship, frequently ran the London–Melbourne route in the 1850s and by 1860, while the Peninsular & Oriental Steam Company (P&O) dominated long-distance passenger business to Australia. Liner shipping conferences and agreements between steamship companies in Australian overseas trade existed from the 1880s, which were mainly under British control. Mergers and combinations of shipping companies over the next few decades usually favored British rather than Australian investors and by the end of the First World War, Lord Inchcape's leadership of merged companies – including P&O – gave Britain unrivaled power over Australian coastal, regional and intercontinental trades.

After the Second World War major changes occurred in Australia's deployment of shipping and it was now that they flourished under Australian ownership, especially the large ships that carried minerals, and the tankers that transported crude oil for large corporations. The major Australian owned company in the coastal trade was the Australian National Line. By the 1970s containerization had become an important part of Australia's shipping industry with roll-on roll-off cargoes revolutionizing the landscape of ports. By 1997 the largest carriers could lift over 6,000 containers with about 70,000 tons of freight. The growth of commercial airlines led to a decline in passenger liners but they were often redeployed into the mass business of cruising at sea. Specialized vessels including refrigerated fruit carriers and car carriers have also thrived at Australian ports since the 1970s.

External commerce has drawn Australia into a wider trading world that is essential for the economic livelihood of its citizens. The remoteness of the first European settlements made long-distance trade problematic: ships could take the best part of a year to sail from Sydney to London. This 'tyranny of distance' was eventually overcome in the mid-19th century by steam navigation and communication improvements made possible by the electric cable telegraph, but the vast distance from Europe still made it imperative that Australians find suitable products to ship to Europe in exchange for the manufactured products of Britain's Industrial Revolution. Before the 1820s whaling and sealing were prosperous maritime trades in Australian waters but by the 1840s both trades had declined due to new laws enacted by the government.

The rapid growth of the pastoral frontier in New South Wales and Australia Felix between 1820 and 1850 led to a surge in wool exports, which comprised over two-thirds of colonial Australia's total export income by 1850. Wool remained the leading export from Australia to the mother country for generations apart from gold, which surpassed it after 1851 for two decades. The introduction of the wool press revolutionized the industry by reducing the weight of wool carried by three-quarters. Furthermore, the gold rush of the 1850s produced an important mineral for export. In the 1880s, Australian ships also exported wheat, refrigerated meat and dairy products to Britain. Coal was exported from Australia but it was not until the late 1930s that bulk carriers were built in Australia to carry coal overseas. By the 1960s, Australia's industrialization had enabled a 'seaport industrial machine' to integrate the raw materials and metallurgical industry with bulk carriers.

Australian international trade was not only confined to long-distance connections with Britain, as sandalwood was also exported to China in the 19th century. Tahitian pork was imported from various areas for consumption in Australian homes while tea, sugar and rice were commodities that linked Asia with Australia. On the eve of the First World War France bought more than half of Australia's wool and hides, while Belgium and Germany took most of the zinc and almost half of the copper. Nevertheless, Anglo-Australian commodity trade was still dominant with 60% of Australia's import income coming from the United Kingdom and 44% of Australia's exports being sent to the UK in 1913.

It was only after the Second World War that Anglo-Australian trade gradually declined as a share of total Australian commodity trade. By 1966 the UK provided 22% of Australia's imports and took 13% of Australia's exports by value. This means that Australia now imported more goods from the United States than from Britain and one-third of Australia's exports were dispatched to Japan and other Asian markets. These trade trends accelerated after the UK joined the European Economic Community in 1973 and began to whittle down significant components of its traditional trade with Australia. As a result Asian markets rapidly began to take a larger share of Australia's foreign trade, in fact Asia now accounts by value for over three-quarters of Australia's exports and for around half of Australia's imports.

Politics in Australia Since the 1970s

Various economic reforms were implemented between 1983 and 1996 under the Hawke-Keating Labor administration and they endorsed reforms that caused the fluctuation of the dollar and the relaxation of banking legislation. More reforms were established under the new Liberal-National Coalition Governments from the mid-1990s that included extra taxes and industry systems.

The first female Australian Prime Minister, Julia Gillard was elected in 2010. She had run a successful campaign and won against Kevin Rudd, who was the leader of the Labor Party.

Tony Abbott won the new election in 2013 but was defeated by Malcolm Turnbull in 2016.

Chapter 6: African History

Africa is the second most populated continent and second largest in total land area. It consists of about 6% of the Earth's overall total surface, approximately 30.3 million kilometers including its adjacent islands and is inhabited by over 1.1 billion people, about 15% of the world's human population. The Mediterranean Sea marks the extent of Africa's northern reaches, while the Red Sea, Suez Canal, and the Sinai Peninsula are positioned in the northeast. The Indian Ocean is located to the southeast and the Atlantic Ocean lies to the west.

Within Africa there is a vast diversity of ethnicities, cultures and languages, as the continent is well known for its fantastic ancient societies and cultures. Since the continent possesses a lot of minerals and natural resources it was colonized by the European powers in the 19th century. However, in present times, most states have gone through the process of decolonization that mainly took place in the 20th century.

Ancient Civilizations
The most famous ancient civilization known to live in African territory is that of ancient Egypt. There are three main early African civilizations: the ancient Egyptians, the Nubians and the Swahili people. Ancient Egypt is known to have been the most developed civilization from among these three.

Ancient Egypt
The ancient Egyptians were located in Northeastern Africa and concentrated along the banks of the river Nile. They kept their society and culture intact for over a thousand years because they used the River Nile, the Mediterranean, and the Red Sea as borders to keep invaders out. The first inhabitants

around the River Nile were Stone-Age people who were hunter-gatherers and found this particular area rich in wildlife. Due to significant changes in climate, these nomads began to settle as farming communities.

The most important part of ancient Egypt was its use of the River Nile. The Nile not only provided communication and a route for trading but also kept the land around it extremely fertile, it became the perfect place for growing different kinds of crops and for building houses. The Nile River is not only the longest river in Africa but is regarded by many as the longest in the world (Some argue that it is the Amazon River in South America). Its origin can be found at the joining of the three rivers that flow from Uganda, Sudan, and Ethiopia. The three rivers meet in southern Egypt and form the Nile that stretches across the whole country until the northern border where it joins with the Mediterranean Sea.

Therefore, Egypt's inhabitants were able to develop into communities because of the existence of this river. They had originally settled on the rich ground along the banks of the Nile to utilize it as a water source in the harsh desert environment that exists in northern Africa. The Egyptian territory was split into two regions: the flat flood plains in the north by the sea, and the narrow river valleys in the south. Along with the Red Sea the Nile enabled the ancient Egyptians to control both western and eastern trade.

The river also provided these early inhabitants with clay, which they sundried in a brick form to construct their buildings. This kind of block lasted a long time because the external surface was made from hard stone and protected them from the winds and the sun. Egypt also had a wide variety of rocks that facilitated the development of grand architecture made from a combination of clay bricks and stone. Egypt only experienced the spring and summer seasons so the ruling class used farmers to help build the planned architecture during the months of flooding.

The ancient Egyptians believed in almost the same religion throughout their entire existence. They were polytheistic in nature and powerful priests, funded by Pharaohs, organized their religion. The Pharaoh was considered to be God's second in command and controlled all political affairs of the people. Moreover, the Egyptians believed in life after death so they performed lengthy rituals to embalm the deceased in preparation for its needs. Only nobles were honored with these ceremonies because of the time and effort required, once embalmed they were placed in individual chambers inside large pyramids along with all of their possessions from their worldly life. These rituals eventually led to the construction of great pyramids and monuments that are famous even up until today.

The Egyptians had a stately society in which the great priest established all social and working relations by the permission of the Pharaoh. The Pharaoh was not only God's representative on Earth but was also considered to be a priest and a king. He or she owned all of the land and chose to distribute it as they saw fit. The nobles, priests, members of the royal family and appointed ministers were free from the hard work that was reserved for the peasants and slaves. Children inherited the same social class as their parents so there was no possibility of changing class or moving up the hierarchy unless the Pharaoh made an exception. The lower classes cultivated crops and were mostly employed in the construction of large monuments and pyramids. The upper classes made significant contributions to the study of mathematics and writing, some of which are still used today.

Nubia

The Nubian civilization was also located near the River Nile in what parts of what is now modern day Sudan and Egypt. As the people lived side by side with the ancient Egyptians they shared a lot of similar practices, including the construction of pyramids. The Nubian region was known as the Ta-Seti Kingdom and it ruled in Egypt from 712 to 657 BC. After the Egyptians had regained their independence from the Nubians, the Nubians continued their civilization for over 100 years in Sudan. Also, this culture is well known for its advancements in language and writing, as many people translated several religious books and kept a written record of their laws, rites and religion.

The region in which the Nubians lived was rich in gold, ivory, and ebony. However, the climate was very harsh because rains were infrequent, so because many could not survive in the harsh climate, the Nubians were less in number than the Egyptians. The Nubian civilization converted to Christianity in 540 AD and they are believed to be one of the first civilizations in the Middle East to spread Christianity throughout the region.

Swahili civilization

The Swahili civilization was located on the east African coast and existed for more than a thousand years. This culture sprang from when some locals mixed with foreign traders, who were mostly known to be Arabs. Consequently, the culture and language that emerged was a mixed form called Swahili. The term means 'people of the coast' in Arabic, because the Swahili people lived in coastal towns. This location was easy to trade for the Arabs and others who travelled long distances from different parts of the world. Each coastal town was independent of others and differentiated itself from the Nubians and the ancient Egyptians. Therefore, the Swahilis did not have a single kingdom of their own and their towns consisted of stonewall buildings similar to those of the Arabs, buildings further inland, however, possessed a mixture of African and Arabic styles. The people from the Swahili civilization adopted the Islamic religion several centuries after it began in the 7th century.

Carthage

Carthage was a Phoenician city-state that included the Carthaginian Empire between the 7th and 3rd century BCE. It was located on the north coast of Africa and was founded by the Phoenicians of Tyre in 814 BC when the Phoenicians selected this geographical spot for several reasons. First of all, the quality of its harbor and its proximity to trading routes was incredibly convenient, secondly, the environment was ideal because the city was built on a triangular peninsula that was covered with small hills and backed by a lake. Finally, Carthage had easy access to the Mediterranean, was shielded from the violent storms on the coasts and could be easily defended.

Carthaginians were also known as the Punic people. The interests of these people were economic and commercial, whereas other cities of the ancient world tended to focus more on the arts and architecture. As a result there is not much to show in terms of Punic literature, libraries or archives.

Carthage controlled most of the expensive part of the Western trade and later, during Roman times, Punic elements such as furniture were considered extravagant and were often copied by the people. The richness of Carthage came mainly from the exploitation of silver mines in North Africa, which were created when the city was founded. During this early time Carthaginian territorial claims suffered from the Sicilian Wars, the Pyrrhic War, and the Punic Wars.

After its foundation Carthage enjoyed considerable economic success due to its trade, and this resulted in the construction of a powerful navy. The Phoenicians' growth in power initiated a conflict with the Greeks located in Syracuse, because they also wanted to control the Mediterranean Sea and its trade. Therefore, Sicily became a focus of their struggle as both empires wanted to use the island for economic and political growth. The Greeks and the Phoenicians had already established colonies in the territory and were constantly fighting each other. The first Sicilian war occurred in 480 BC when Gelo the Athenian leader of Syracuse attempted to force the island under his rule. Carthage lost the war because there was corruption among the armed forces and their general Hamilcar Barca made some serious mistakes on the battlefield.

As a consequence of this loss the nobles negotiated amongst themselves and a republic was established. In 409 BC the second Sicilian War occurred, but by this time Carthage had recovered from the first war and conquered new territories, such as modern-day Tunisia and several other areas in North Africa. Carthage wished to rule the island of Sicily so its army attacked again in the hope of reconquering what was once theirs. The battle was constant and several times the fight swung in favor of Carthage, but the army was laid low by a series of plagues. For several years the struggle for Sicily continued between the Greeks and the Phoenicians. The last Sicilian War occurred in 315 BC when the Tyrant of Syracuse attempted to take over the last remaining Carthaginian territories. The Carthaginian army fought back with all of its might but the Greeks ultimately took control and emerged as victors, however, the Carthaginians still kept pockets of land under their control.

The Pyrrhic war is another critical event that took place throughout this region between 280 and 275 BC. The war was fought mainly against Pyrrhus, who was the king of Greece at the time. Pyrrhus was determined to fight until he had full control of the lands around him because he wanted to stop the emerging power of the Roman Republic. Pyrrhus desired Sicily very much, so he fought in order to remove the Carthaginians entirely, but the Pyrrhus campaigns were inconclusive so the situation remained as it had for Carthage.

Over the 3rd and 2nd century BC this city was engaged in a series of wars with Rome often known as the Punic Wars. This succession of wars ended in 146 BC, when Carthage finally fell and was absorbed into the Roman Empire. It was now that the Roman Senate attempted to establish a colony on this particular site but failed until 29 BC when Augustus established the African government of the empire. Later Carthage grew prosperous and became very famous, but in the middle of the 3rd century the city started to decline.

In terms of their beliefs, and although there were some small Jewish communities, the Carthaginians based their religious practices on Phoenician religion, which meant a majority of the people were polytheists. They worshipped various local gods and believed in a supreme divine couple named Tanit and Ba'al Hammon.

Great Zimbabwe Empire

The Zimbabwe kingdom was a medieval empire that was situated in modern-day Zimbabwe. The capital of this kingdom was Great Zimbabwe and was known for its large stone structures, in fact the origin of the word Zimbabwe comes from two possible terms that together mean "stone house." The kingdom declined in the 15th century, but the stone constructions in the city are still standing. UNESCO has named the site of remaining structures as a World Heritage Site.

This location was inhabited in the 11th century when the people from Mapungubwe, who lived in southern Africa, settled the Zimbabwe plateau. The land was full of new possibilities because the plains were vast and fertile so the people took advantage of farming, herding and the mining of various minerals such as gold, iron and copper. Thus, the location became an ideal place for trading. The kingdom of Zimbabwe was established in 1220 and the last records that could be found say the kingdom was inhabited until the 16th century. The territory of the kingdom extended from the Limpopo River and the Zambezi River to Mozambique and Botswana. It is also known to have covered the Transvaal area of northern South Africa.

The kingdom of Zimbabwe was a monarchy with an established rigid three-tier class structure that had more than 150 tributary headquarters in other minor cities. The kingdom of Zimbabwe commanded a bigger rule than the Mapungubwe, the Butuan, and the Mutapa. Not everyone agrees on the origin of the rulers of Zimbabwe but there is evidence that suggests they were also known as the Karanga, an arm of the Shona people. The pottery of the Karanga is also very similar to that of the Zimbabwe region, but another theory suggests the people of Zimbabwe descended from a community that lived in Kopje, less than a hundred miles away from the location of Great Zimbabwe, but from wherever they came the first inhabitants made a transition from small farming communities to large stratified societies and by 1000 AD the population of the kingdom was divided and ranked by status, from the higher elite, to peasants who worked with cattle.

A large number of rock settlements were built as a result of economic and political growth. These were enormous undertakings were built by the peasants for the king and the elite, such an enterprise meant that there were sophisticated workplaces to design and conduct trades and skills such as those required by blacksmiths. This type of construction became characteristic of the city as people began to create more and more buildings using these rocks, a building practice that had been inherited from the Mapungubwe. The construction of imposing stone buildings reached its climax in the Kingdom of Zimbabwe where they mainly used granite, as this kind of rock predominates in the region.

Consequently the Great Zimbabwe Monument was constructed with granite as well. The method they used to build involved dry-stone walling and demanded a high level of masonry expertise, also, much of the site of the Great Zimbabwe Monument was based on round natural rock formations and had an enclosing wall of 20 meters in height. Inside this monument there are passages that are concentric along with some enclosures and one of them is thought to be the royal enclosure where large quantities of gold and arms could once be found.

In terms of its economy the kingdom controlled gold and ivory trade from the southern coast of Africa as Great Zimbabwe was the center of an international trading system that encompassed many places across Africa and Asia and because the people had an adamant web of trading, Asian and Arabic goods could easily be found in the kingdom. The principal economic activity was derived from having gold, copper and iron, but the people also kept livestock and possessed other small businesses, thus it was that most of the kingdom's wealth came from cattle production and gold. The mines from which they extracted the gold were located more than 40 kilometers away from Great Zimbabwe, although some speculate that rather than having direct control over the mines, the people from Zimbabwe managed to trade cattle for large amounts of gold.

By 1200 the city was well established and became well-known as a religious and trading center. Some say that religion played a crucial part in the kingdom's rise to power while others believe the tall tower was used to worship their gods. The people from Zimbabwe believed in the Shona religion so they worshiped Mwari who was their supreme god. In 1430 Prince Nyatsimba Mutota traveled north in search of salt and other commercial goods and it was here, after a short battle, that he conquered the northern region, which later became known as the Kingdom of Mutapa.

This new kingdom grew aggressively through successful trade and became an economic power of its day. In 1450 it eventually eclipsed Zimbabwe entirely, as most of the people had now abandoned that territory. The end of the empire resulted in the fragmentation of tribes and two new kingdoms appeared: the Mutua in the north, which kept all of Zimbabwe's administrative structure but not the masonry tradition; and the kingdom of Butua in the south, which was an identical smaller version of the Kingdom of Zimbabwe. Later, both of these kingdoms merged to become the largest and most influential state of the Kalanga states, the Rozwi Empire.

Some theorize that the splitting up of the kingdom of Zimbabwe was due to environmental factors, because the combination of overgrazing and drought caused the soil to become exhausted, what had once been an ideal plain of fertile land became rapidly useless. Others have suggested that the kingdom of Zimbabwe wanted to maximize its gold trade, therefore the people needed to find new trade centers by traveling further across the land to achieve their goals.

The Kingdom of Kongo

The Kingdom of Kongo, situated in west-central Africa, was encompassed by the Atlantic Ocean – west of the Kwango River – all through to the Congo River and north to the Kwanza River. Kongo had several provinces ruled by the Manikongo, known as the king; however, its influence shaped many neighboring kingdoms such as Matamba, Ndongo, Kakongo and others.

The kingdom of Kongo existed as an independent state from 1390 to 1891 and as a state of the kingdom of Portugal from 1891 to 1914. It was officially founded by Lukeni Lua Nimi in 1390.

Before that small Iron Age communities settled north of the Congo River because of the fertile soil, and also due to the abundance of easily accessible iron and copper ores near the river. Over time this small settlement prospered and grew wealthy. By the 15th century many communities had developed into a minor federation of loosely connected towns that then incorporated territories to eventually become a royal patrimony. The capital of Kongo was known as Mbanza Kongo and it became densely populated, which allowed the king to keep his resources close at hand. Furthermore, the kingdom was able to create two principal harbors that became known as Pinda and Sonyo.

People from the Kongo mostly lived on agricultural production, fishing and hunting. The governors were commanded to collect taxes, force labor upon some of the people, and collect fines to continue growth. Due to an abundance of natural resources, new crafts emerged relating to metalworking, pottery and raffia textiles, but it was the ruling class who mainly controlled these activities. The most prolific form of art was demonstrated through the nkisi objects, which were closely related to their religious beliefs. It is interesting to note that the nkisi figures were the only type of art made available to everyone.

The expansion of Kongo territory was mainly achieved through trade and by forming alliances, rather than through military conquests. The power of the Manikongo (the king) was exercised by some governors and there were three leading states in the kingdom: Loango, Ngoyo, and Kakongo. Expeditions were launched in search of new territory when there was an increase in population and more food was needed. Kongo became one of the biggest states in Africa, covering territory from the Atlantic Ocean all the way to the Kwango River.

Kongo's system of Manikongo succession was often problematic because, although the position was generally transferred from father to son, there were often disputes between the sons and brothers of former kings. Kongo had a court where political matters would be discussed and it was supported by an extensive network of civil servants. The court consisted of relatives of the king including the governors of various villages.

Before converting to Christianity the people from the Kongo Kingdom believed in a supreme god named Nzambi. They also believed in intermediary representations, such as the land, the sky and ancestral spirits, all of which were portrayed in nkisi objects. The people often consulted a "nganga" (diviner) if they felt hardship, or felt that they had insulted a spirit. This nganga would usually instruct them to add some medicine into certain nkisi to achieve well-being and recovery.

When the Portuguese arrived in Kongo in 1483 both the Manikongo and his son were baptized and given Christian names and henceforth strong bonds were formed between the kingdom of Kongo and Portugal. Some nobles from Kongo were taken to Portugal and some Portuguese went to live in the kingdom of Kongo. A Roman Catholic Church was built to transmit the Christian religion in the territory and during the years that followed Kongo became the primary source of slaves, not just for Portugal, but for most of Europe.

The Portuguese were primarily attracted by the gold mines the Kongo possessed. This relationship that they had formed with the people of Kongo enabled them to exploit and trade those goods, and due to their lust and greed for more slaves and gold, the Portuguese ended up disrupting the peace they had forged with the people of Kongo and they were expelled from the territory in 1526. However, the Jagas invaded the kingdom of Kongo in 1568 and the Kongo people were forced to ask the Portuguese for help. From that time on the Kongo kingdom never regained power and after struggles with the Portuguese it was finally colonized in 1885.

Colonization by Europe

During the 19th century Africa went through significant change. It experienced famine, disease and power struggles among the ruling class, and African leaders made alliances with merchants and missionaries from Europe to accomplish their own goals and ambitions. The Europeans took advantage of these alliances to later conquer the territories in Africa.

During the first years of the century Europe had little knowledge about the African Continent's inner regions. The Europeans focused on trading along the coast, while African and Arab merchants handled the domestic goods and slaves. By the end of the century Europe had succeeded in executing a consistent colonization plan that reached its peak in the 1880's.

In 1807, with the British abolition of slave trade, the British navy began patrolling the African coasts and intercepting any other nation's slave ships. European oppression continued in the last two decades of the century when conflicts and rivalries between the continents began to significantly impact the people living there. During the 1880's, European powers divided African territory among themselves seemingly not aware of how much land they had taken without the consent of the inhabitants.

When the First World War broke out in 1914 the African people played a major role and helped the Allied Powers. As we mentioned before, the early European expeditions to Africa consisted of colonizing uninhabited islands or establishing coastal ports as a base of trade. During these first years, the

European interest in Africa was strictly commercial and economical as they focused on making establishing routes.

However, a major European intervention occurred in Africa in the 19th century, a moment that became known as the "Scramble for Africa", because the leading European powers divided African lands amongst themselves. This scramble took place at a conference in 1884 where the main powers in Europe established international guidelines for the acquisition of African territory. The conference formalized what is now known as "New Imperialism" where Europe added almost 9 million square miles of overseas colonies to its territory. One-fifth of the globe was now made up of European Colonies including the territories of Africa.

Europe's plans for Africa provoked considerable political and diplomatic responses from African leaders, who eventually resorted to military resistance. This resistance had two primary forms: guerrilla warfare – often used by small-scale, decentralized societies – and direct military engagement that was most commonly used by centralized state systems.

European powers sent agents to sign treaties of protection with the leaders of African nations, kingdoms and societies. These agreements often had clauses that the African leaders did not agree to, which resulted in military resistance. The Europeans thought that the Africans had signed their sovereignty away, but the Africans thought the treaties only added up to diplomatic and commercial deals. After discovering the truth, African leaders felt betrayed by the European powers who had been trying to impose political and economic authority on their territories.

The European powers were made up of Britain, Portugal and France, which claimed for themselves regions in both Africa and Asia. Similarly, emerging powers – such as Germany and Italy – followed suit, all be it on a smaller scale. At the time European states felt that there was a pressing need to grow politically and economically so possessing vast chunks of territory seemed to be an absolute necessity in lieu of what they had planned for their nations. European powers were driven by lust and greed for both economic and political growth, which resulted in competition and a constant struggle between the colonies and even the powers themselves.

The colonizing nations used strategic government policies whereby the French, Portuguese, Germans and the Belgians exercised their control through a system of centralized government known as "direct rule." For example, France ruled its African colonies from France and appointed chiefs individually considering their loyalty to the nation only and it was through this system that they were able to establish large colonies in Africa such as French West Africa and the French Equatorial Africa colonies. France assigned officials, passed laws and approved any type of statute before it could be passed by colonial assemblies.

The Germans had struggled over the years with their colonies, with local groups living on their African territory resisting enforced labor and taxation. In 1888 the Germans were almost expelled from their territory due to their meddling. Nearly ten years later, when the land seemed conquered, they still struggled with government centers and small military fortresses. In 1905 there was an uprising in the area and it was suppressed by German soldiers who were forced to use machine guns. For the next few years the struggle continued with armed intervention.

Belgium called their colony the Congo Free State, which meant that those residing in the region only followed the orders of King Leopold II. The treatment of the locals was extremely harsh and other powers suggested that the king should control the work done in the territory, after some years, the area was annexed as another Belgian Colony.

An alternative system, such as that implemented by the British, saw control asserted upon their colonies by what is called "indirect rule." This meant that they identified local power holders and encouraged them to govern in favor of the British Empire. The British colonies were split into provinces or states that were governed by provincial commissioners and they were further divided into districts that were led by district commissioners. Laws, policies on taxation, mining and agricultural production were popular subjects of discussion in London. Then, when a decision was made, laws or policies were passed to the lower colonial administrative levels for enforcement.

The European powers paid a great deal of attention to the economics of colonization. They acquired land, forced labor, introduced cash crops, changed trading patterns and added foreign labor, all aiming to have a positive impact on the bottom line. As a result Africa became a great source of raw material for European industry. Eventually, the colonial powers abolished slavery, developed infrastructure and improved both education and healthcare.

Decolonization

By 1905 European powers had gained control of most of the African continent. However, there were two exceptions: Liberia, which had been populated by African-American former slaves, and Ethiopia, which had resisted colonization by Italy. France and Great Britain possessed the most African colonies but Germany, Spain, Belgium, Italy and Portugal had their own colonies as well. With colonialism the African leaders not only lost power over their territories, but also any control over their natural resources such as gold and rubber.

Decolonization occurred with the withdrawal of European powers from their territories in Africa and the colonies were able to regain political and economic independence. The decolonization of Africa took place following the Second World War, when most of the territories broke free from European rule. During the Cold War the people from any remaining colonies organized independence movements and colonial powers eventually withdrew their control from African territory.

The first step toward decolonization took place in 1941 when the United States President, Franklin D. Roosevelt, and British Prime Minister, Winston Churchill, met to discuss how to begin the process of freeing Africa. They created a document known as the Atlantic Charter, which became very popular amongst politicians. Roosevelt introduced the concept of independence of the imperial colonies after considerable consideration.

When World War II ended, the United States and the African Colonies pressured Britain to follow the terms stated in the Atlantic Charter. Some British people considered the African colonies to be of little use and so they eventually introduced democratic governments at a local level in the colonies so that the people could finally rule themselves once more.

Chapter 7 – World War I & II and the Vietnam War

World War I

There are various reasons – including political and military tensions – that led to World War I. The main reason often cited involves the assassination of Archduke Franz Ferdinand of Austria-Hungary when he visited Sarajevo in Bosnia on June 28, 1914. A man named Princip, who was a member of a terrorist group called the Black Hand, assassinated him; he also had his own political motives for the assassination. Princip and his gang members were frustrated by the fact that Serbs in Bosnia did not have their own government and blamed the Austrian-Hungarian government for creating such a situation.

After the assassination, a period of time known as the July Crisis occurred, in which Germany, Britain, Austria-Hungary, France and Russia all went through sensitive political movements. Austria-Hungary issued a series of demands known as the July Ultimatum to Serbia on July 23rd and declared that Austria-Hungary would enter Serbia with its military to investigate the death of the Archduke. The Serbian government read all of the terms of the ultimatum and refused the military intervention Austria-Hungary had requested. This caused the first country to declare war; a war that eventually spread around the entire globe.

Officially, World War I began on July 28, 1914 when Austria-Hungary declared war on Serbia and although it originated between these two small countries, it soon spread throughout the rest of Europe to France, Great Britain, Russia, and Germany. It spread to all of these nations because they had formed various treaties with one another that forced them to aid their allied nations. As a result, frontlines were quickly established across the Austrian-Hungarian and German borders.

The Western and Eastern Fronts

Within the first four weeks of the declaration of war the frontlines saw powerful assaults and quick movements by both sides. France and Belgium were both attacked initially by Germany, while Austria-Hungary and Germany were attacked by Russia. Serbia was of course attacked by Austria-Hungary, since that is where the conflict had first erupted. After the Battle of the Marne between the fifth and ninth of September 1914, the Western Front was established in the center of France, where they would mostly stay for the entirety of the war. In the east, the Eastern Front also developed into what seemed to be a permanent border.

The Ottoman Empire

While France, Germany, Great Britain, and others had commenced fighting, the Ottoman Empire was dragged into the midst of battle because Germany had manipulated Russia into believing the Ottomans had launched attacks on them. Furthermore, Russia wanted to secure the Dardanelles, since it was a waterway that was valuable to Russia but was located on the Gallipoli Peninsula, within the Ottoman Empire. When Russia attacked the Ottoman Empire, France and Britain were forced to help its ally. However, they failed in their attacks on the Dardanelles and removed their armies from the region after several months.

Trench Warfare

Between 1916 and 1917 trench warfare took its toll on both fronts, where soldiers dug out trenches to fire at the enemy mostly with machine guns, heavy artillery and chemical weaponry. The area in between the trenches was covered in mines and it was extremely dangerous to be caught in 'no man's land'. Millions of soldiers died in these trenches and neither side gained any real advantage over the other.

Arrival of the United States and Russia's Departure

On both the eastern and western frontlines the European armies found themselves at a grinding impasse. Things only began to change when American troops, or Doughboys as they were known, began to arrive in the spring of 1917, angered by German attacks on its shipping the US joined forces with Britain against Germany. Russia was forced to abandon the war when the Bolshevik Revolution burst onto the streets of Petrograd.

The End of the War and the Armistice

In 1918 both sides commenced with their ultimate strategies and last resorts to win the war, but neither side was successful. Germany lost a succession of battles against a tired Allied force and was forced to retreat. Influenza spread amongst both sides and killed many soldiers, while internal revolts broke out in both the German and Austrian-Hungarian governments.

On November 11th 1918 – with other members of the Central Powers having signed previous agreements – an armistice was agreed with the Allies final opponent, Germany. On the completion of the Treaty of Versailles on January 10th 1920 – when it formally came into effect – the Austro-Hungarian was no more, and the Allies, blaming Germany for the war's outbreak, had imposed what came to be seen as impossible penalties upon the Germans. These severe limitations and sanctions set out in the Treaty only sowed the seeds of bitterness and anger of later conflict.

Germany After the War

Numerous historians agree that the punishments Germany faced via the Treaty of Versailles were far too strict. Instead of bringing peace back to Europe it only helped to bring about the outbreak of the Second World War. The German people felt embarrassed to discuss the war and were forced to pay reparations they could not afford. Although the nation only paid a fraction of what it was meant to pay, it caused a huge strain on the economy. In the next few years, with increasing amounts of friction between Germany and the other European nations, extremist groups like the Nazis were able to take advantage of the situation.

World War II

With Adolf Hitler having become Chancellor of Germany on January 30 1933, conflict seemed inevitable, no matter how hard other leaders tried to avoid hostilities Hitler simply demanded more, until in September 1939 he launched his invasion of Poland. World War Two had begun.

Britain ordered Germany to leave the territory they had invaded but Germany refused. In retaliation France and Britain reluctantly declared war on Germany but did not launch any military campaigns immediately. In the following year, Germany attacked Norway, Denmark, France, the Netherlands and Belgium. Because Germany had strategically planned its attacks, all of these countries fell to their strategy of blitzkrieg (lightening war) one after the other.

German Invasion of Poland

The Nazi-Soviet Non-Aggression Pact was signed on August 23, 1939 and it allowed Hitler to pursue his ambitions without fear of Russian interference. Hitler had already planned to destroy Poland and to subjugate its people to his will. The first attack on Poland began at 4.45 am on Friday, September 1st, 1939. The Germans swept all resistance aside via their strategy of blitzkrieg; they had no intention of reliving the horrors of the First World War, with its trenches and meaningless stalemates. They fully utilized all and any military technological advances, coordinated attacks, and abrasive speed to gain victory wherever possible. The German forces also employed brutality, terror, summary executions and merciless aggression against sections of the civilian population.

Neville Chamberlain, having become Britain's Conservative prime minister in 1937, had signed an agreement with Poland guaranteeing assistance if they were attacked. When Hitler invaded Poland Britain was forced to declare war on Germany on September 3rd, with the French following six hours later. In a last vain attempt at securing peace the British sent planes carrying leaflets to drop among the German population to encourage them to stand up against Hitler so the war could be stopped before significant bloodshed.

On September 17th the German war machine advanced towards Warsaw. The Soviet Union had secretly agreed to aid Germany by signing the Non-Aggression Pact and thus attacked Poland from the east. Crushed between two totalitarian heavyweights, Poland crumbled within a short period of time and Warsaw was forced to surrender to Germany on September 27th. The Germans and Russians had agreed to split up Poland prior to the invasion, so once they had full control they razed the villages, massacred the inhabitants and caused serious destruction. In towns such as Lodz, Jews were herded into ghettos and transported to concentration camps. Hitler visited Warsaw on the 5th of October and upon seeing the devastated capital, declared: 'This is how I deal with any European city'.

Finnish-Soviet War

Stalin knew that his country's pact with Germany would not last indefinitely so he sought a buffer to protect his nation against any future German attack. By June 1940 he had bullied Estonia, Latvia and Lithuania into cooperating with his demands, demands that eventually led to full annexation. However, when Finland resisted and refused to submit to the Soviets so began the 105-day 'Winter War', with Russia attacking Finland on November 30th, 1939. Russia expected an easy victory, as the Germans had experienced against the Poles, but were surprised by their opponents. The Finnish army fought bravely and showed expertise in guerrilla warfare to such an extent that it was difficult for the Soviets to defeat the Finnish. Historians state that Stalin had purged the military in the 1930s and thereby negatively impacted his army. Along with poor equipment that froze in the plummeting temperatures, the Soviets learned a hard but useful lesson. They were only eventually able to subdue the Finns in March of 1940 by sheer weight of numbers alone.

Norwegian Campaign

The supply of iron from Sweden to Germany through the northern Norwegian port of Narvik was vital to the German army. When the British found out, they decided to destroy the supply source but the Germans feared losing this resource and marched towards Narvik to secure it. On April 8th, 1940, when the British boats began laying mines off the Norwegian drift, Chamberlain crowed that Hitler had "missed the bus."

Be that as it may, the Germans progressed quickly into Scandinavia and drove Denmark to a fast surrender. Neutral Norway was forced to fight, but Norwegian ports tumbled to the Germans one after the other. The British reaction, albeit quick, was poorly planned because the troops had arrived in Norway without skis and only had a set of traveler maps at their disposal. When Germany attacked Holland and Belgium on the 10th of May the British evacuated Norway and moved into the Low Countries. Norway eventually fell under German control and the levers of power were given to the Norwegian Nazi Vidkun Quisling.

After the Norwegian disaster Chamberlain, in the midst of yelling from the House of Commons, was expelled by the government because he was not able to form a coalition government. Winston Churchill, previously the First Lord of the Admiralty, assumed responsibilities in his place. On the same day of May 10th Hitler unleashed more lightening assaults that caused immediate damaged to the Allied Forces.

Chamberlain died from cancer six months after being removed from his post and is not remembered so fondly by some of the British public.

War for France

The period between the beginning of the war and the 10th of May 1940 is referred to as the 'phony war' in Britain because the actual war still appeared to be far away. During this time the young were transported to countryside and rations were stored in preparation for war. The people experienced many black outs and were forced to use gas lamps.

Belgium was being overpowered by the Germans and only after begging the Allies for help did Britain and France respond by moving into Belgium to counter the German assault. Along the Franco-German border the French had placed a weaker force because they had put such confidence in the Maginot Line, which was a 280-mile long line of fortifications built in the mid-1930s to protect France against Germany. The Germans rendered it useless one morning in May 1940 when they evaded it easily by simply rounding the north of its furthest reaches. They marched right through the Ardennes forests and surprised everyone because the French had considered the terrain to be too extreme for the Germans to cross. On May 14 the Germans took the town of Sedan on the French side of the Ardennes and did not even stop to think about French resistance as they pushed north towards the English Channel. The Allies were forced to regroup and rethink their strategy since they had expected the German forces to march towards Paris. During the First World War in 1916, the Germans were not able to take Verdun despite ten months of horrendous trench fighting, but in May 1940 it had taken them one day.

In Holland, Rotterdam, continuously shelled, saw no hope of victory, and so the Dutch finally surrendered in fear of further destruction on May 15th. When Belgium also surrendered on May 28 the Allied Forces were caught with their backs to the water in the French town of Dunkirk. The Germans were ready to demolish the entire British Expeditionary Force but were mysteriously requested to halt by Hitler just outside the town. Between May 26th and June 3rd more than 1,000 military and nonmilitary vessels saved 338,226 troops by taking them back to Britain across the English Channel. The retreat occurred within the grip of a horrible frenzy, with broken ranks and mayhem ensuing, so much so that officers shot some of their soldiers for losing their restraint instead of retreating in a orderly manner. Meanwhile, Hitler's officers watched, wondering as to why they had been ordered to wait.

On the 4th of June Churchill refused to acknowledge the 'miracle of Dunkirk' as a triumph in the House of Commons and referred to it as 'deliverance' instead. He conveyed his famous 'We shall fight on the beaches' speech, ending with the interminable words, 'We shall never surrender.' Be that as it may, the French saw the retreat differently and considered it to be a colossal betrayal since Paris was lost, now surrounded by German forces.

On the 10th of June Italy proclaimed war on the Allies and Hitler's forces entered an evacuated Paris, four days after more than 2 million of its citizens had fled south in fear of being massacred. Before long the swastika fluttered from the Arc de Triomphe as a symbol of Hitler's victory.

On the 16th of June Charles de Gaulle, a French General, escaped France to live as an outcast in London. Although he was declared dead by the Vichy government, he lived for a long time and did not die until November 9, 1970. From London, de Gaulle stated: 'France has lost a battle, however, France has not lost the war... the fire of French resistance must not and shall not die.' His words turned into a call to arms, a demand to continue fighting the war by the remaining French forces.

On June 16th Prime Minister Paul Reynaud of France surrendered and was replaced by Marshal Philippe Pétain, a hero from the 1916 Battle of Verdun. Pétain's first decision was to seek peace negotiations with the Germans and to request Reynaud's capture. On June 22nd the French formally surrendered to the Germans, fifty miles north of Paris. Ironically this took place in a similar area to where the Germans had been forced to surrender in 1918 at the end of the First World War. The railroad carriage along with landmarks celebrating the 1918 victory were destroyed at Hitler's request, whereupon he went to Paris for a tour of the city. On seeing Napoleon's tomb, he stated: 'That was the greatest and finest moment of my life.' Before withdrawing, he requested the decimation of two World War I landmarks including a dedication to Edith Cavell, who was a British attendant shot by the Germans in October 1915.

Hitler now ruled Pétain and his manikin government from the little town of Vichy in France. The Vichy government effectively did the Nazis' ugly work for them, first by directing a horrendous attack upon the French Resistance and then by implementing various laws that saw Jews transported to concentration and death camps.

In July 1940 Churchill founded the Special Operations Executive (SOE) to help the resistance in France. In October 1940 a meeting was scheduled between Pétain and Hitler in which Hitler wished for the French forces to be used against Britain. Although Pétain evaded Hitler's requests during the meeting, photos of the two men standing together were taken and spread across Europe like wildfire. This came as a confirmation that the Vichy government had indeed formed a pact with the Nazis.

In July 1940 Churchill issued a final letter to the chief naval officer of the French navy, which was docked at Mers-el-Kebir in Algeria at the time. The letter stated that the flotilla should be handed over to the British or abandoned, because they had to be kept away from the German naval force or Kriegsmarine. When the chief naval officer declined, Churchill ordered the Royal Navy to fire, and 1297 French mariners were killed. This caused any pretense of friendly relations between the Vichy government and Britain to come to an end.

The Germans took control of the Channel Islands from June 30, 1940 until the German surrender in May 1945, but there always seemed to be one German soldier for every two islanders throughout the war. The islands were not of any strategic significance, but Germany wished to take control of them from the British. Rations became scarce after the Normandy invasion of June 1944 and despite the fact that a few supply ships got past the British, both the Germans and the islanders were on the verge of starvation.

The Battle of Britain
Germany launched air attacks on Great Britain in the middle of 1940 and began what became known as the Battle of Britain. Germany failed miserably in this battle because the British Royal Air Force proved to be far stronger than what the German forces had expected.

With Poland, Norway, Denmark, Belgium, Holland, and France under Nazi control, Britain confronted the German surge alone. Germany's codename for the invasion of Britain was Operation Sea Lion, which Hitler unobtrusively announced on the 16th of July. He declared that the German Air Force, the Luftwaffe, was to destroy the British Royal Air Force as a prelude to an all-out invasion. The next day Hitler issued Britain a peace offering, which he called his 'last appeal to reason.' He said: 'It can only end in the annihilation for one of us. Mr. Churchill thinks it will be Germany. I know it will be

Britain.' Many in Parliament were tempted to accept the offer of peace but Churchill refused.

Hitler's air assault, and thus the Battle of Britain, began on the 13th of August 1940, known as the "Day of the Eagle.' On this day alone 1,485 German airplanes assaulted Britain's coastal landing strips and caused serious damage through advanced fighting. During the following month the RAF and the Luftwaffe battled over the fields of southeast England. A series of dogfights occurred where the normal lifespan of a British pilot was considered to be four to five weeks. Be that as it may, the RAF had the advantage of flying over home ground: if a British pilot needed to be rescued, he could parachute onto British soil at almost any time. On the other hand, the German pilots who landed were captured and imprisoned upon landing. Furthermore, the British were using radar – which gave advance warning of where and when enemy planes would attack – and had broken Germany's Enigma codes at Bletchley Park in Buckinghamshire. As a result, Bletchley Park knew about Operation Sea Lion well before a large number of Hitler's officers did and the RAF always seemed to know exactly where and when the Germans were coming in for an attack.

On August 23rd, a Luftwaffe pilot got lost while coming back from a fight over Britain and erroneously bombed Croydon on the edge of London. The RAF retaliated by bombing Berlin on August 25th, and although there was very limited damage done in the attack, Hitler became incensed and issued the order to bomb London. Between September 1940 and May 16th, 1941, London's population and other British urban areas, even as far north as Glasgow in Scotland, suffered the German aerial onslaught that came to be known as the Blitz.

After May 1941 the Luftwaffe's resources were redirected to support the war raging against the Soviet Union, but not before 440 German planes dropped more than 1,000 tons of explosives on Coventry on the night of November 14, 1940. They caused devastation: 568 individuals were killed and 863 seriously wounded. During the entirety of the Blitz more than 40,000 mainly civilians were killed and approximately 50,000 were wounded. Hitler's goal was to destroy the resolve of the British, but the plan backfired, because they became more determined than ever before to stick it out, even getting the chance to speak with the King and queen consort as they walked among the local people in London. After Buckingham Palace had been hit, the queen consort, Elizabeth, stated: 'I'm glad we've been bombed. It makes me feel I can look the East End in the face.'

Because Hitler was targeting civilians the RAF took advantage of time to regroup and get ready for the next attack. The next German attack occurred on September 15th, now known as the Battle of Britain. The Luftwaffe believed that the RAF was severely weakened and took the opportunity to launch a focused attack on Southeast England. Their plan failed when the RAF destroyed many of the Luftwaffe's aircraft, bringing the Battle of Britain to come to an end. After two days, on seeing he had limited resources to pursue another attack, Hitler put off Operation Sea Lion indefinitely. Churchill is known to have commended those pilots who flew their RAF aircraft against the Luftwaffe by stating, 'Never in the field of human conflict was so much owed by so many to so few.'

Greece and North Africa

Italy, being Germany's ally in the war, launched invasions on North Africa and Greece. When Italy failed to take Greece on its own in 1941 it was forced to ask Germany for help.

Benito Mussolini came to power in 1922 and readily supported the idea of a dictatorship, seeing himself as "Caesar" of Italy. In his attempt to begin building a kingdom deserving of his old antecedents, Italy took for itself Ethiopia (known as Abyssinia at the time) in 1936 and Albania in 1939. On May 16th, 1940, Churchill had pleaded with Mussolini not to declare war: 'Is it too late to stop a river of blood from flowing between the British and Italian peoples?' The plea went ignored by Mussolini who said 'One moment on a battlefield is worth a thousand years of peace.' Italy declared war on the Allies on June 10th when France was on the verge of surrendering. It is theorized that Mussolini only joined the war when he saw that Germany would win. When Hitler heard the news, he remarked: 'First they were too cowardly to take part. Now they are in a hurry so that they can share in the spoils.'

Italy attacked Greece on October 28 from their military base in Albania, but Mussolini's fantasies of empire came crashing down when his army was forced to retreat. With inadequate weapons and the absence of winter attire, the Italians struggled to take Greece. The British came to Greece's aid and together they were able to force the Italians to withdraw to Albania. However, the Greeks now confronted a much graver threat, the Germans.

The Germans invaded Greece on April 6, 1941 and Greece surrendered on April 23rd, their Prime Minister shooting himself as the swastika flew over the Acropolis. The British force in Greece pulled back to Crete, which was then attacked by the Nazis and the British were yet again forced to retreat. The Greeks suffered horrendously under the Germans, many starved to death, and only 2% of Greece's Jewish population survived the war.

Romania's supply of oil was crucial to the German war machine so in September 1940, Germany dismissed Romania's monarch while lending support to a rightist government that began an energetic crusade against its Jewish population. In November 1940 Romania joined the Axis Powers and initiated an attack against the Soviet Union in June of 1941.

In March 1941 Yugoslavia signed the Tripartite Pact with Germany, Italy, and Japan. But after a rebellion – in which Prince Paul was ousted from office – the people repealed the Pact the next day. Enraged, Hitler ordered the destruction of Yugoslavia. On April 6, Belgrade was flattened and about 4,000 people were murdered by April 12; however, the rest of Yugoslavia fought the Germans under the leadership of social partisans who were driven by Josip 'Tito' Broz. Although the Chetnik rebels did not agree with the social partisans' ideology, they still helped in the fight against the Nazis.

It took the Axis powers just eleven days to take full command after surrender, here the Germans gave Croatia their freedom as a rightist republic and the Croatian government began to kill the Jews who lived among them as a result.

Mussolini's experience in North Africa proved just as unprofitable as the one he had undertaken on the European side of the Mediterranean, because when Italian forces attacked British-controlled Egypt from their bases in Libya on September 13, 1940 the British and Commonwealth powers – although unfathomably outnumbered – still ran the Italians out of Egypt. They advanced into Libya and took various coastal towns including Tobruk, a vital town in the war that changed hands several times before forces were withdrawn from the area. The British Prime Minister wanted to separate Libya's capital Tripoli from the war, but with the Greeks being bombarded by the Germans, he was forced to send his troops to help them.

In February of 1941 Hitler sent Erwin Rommel to North Africa to settle matters once and for all. Churchill stated about Erwin Rommel: 'We have a very daring and skillful opponent against us, and may I say, across the havoc of war, a great general.' Over the following two years the Allied Forces fought the Axis Powers in a difficult theater in which the Axis powers were to push the Allies into Egypt and the Allies to push the Axis powers back into Libya. The further one armed force came, the further its supply lines were extended, and so the easier it was for the other to fight back. One thorn in Germany's side was the Mediterranean island of Malta, from where British forces constantly disrupted the German stream of provisions coming from Italy to Tripoli. Despite the serious shelling, Hitler's efforts eventually came to an end and Britain's King George VI awarded the entire island the George Cross.

In June 1942 the British dug themselves in at the little Egyptian town of El Alamein, sixty miles west of Alexandria, when the Germans were 1,400 miles from Tripoli. In July 1942 the decisive battle of El Alamein took place and finished in a stalemate. The second battle, fought by Field Marshal Bernard Montgomery – or 'Monty' as he was known – was a Commonwealth triumph. Rommel was pushed back one tiny bit at a time because his supplies were running out. Eventually, the British, under Monty's command, were able to recapture Tobruk on the 13th of November.

In October 1942 British infantry advanced amid the skirmish of El Alamein while new British and American forces landed in Morocco and Algeria, where, on meeting the Vichy French found them ready to surrender after just three days. Hitler saw their surrender as treachery and reacted by sending troops to the Vichy controlled part of France. Montgomery's men captured Tripoli in January 1943 and after two months made the Germans move westwards into Tunisia. On the 9th of March, Rommel was recalled to Berlin, and it was the Allies who ruptured the reinforced Tunisian-Libyan border with the Germans now effectively pushed into Tunis.

The Germans finally surrendered their North African forces on May 13th 1943, a triumph that led Churchill to state: "Now this is not the end. It is not even the beginning of the end. But it is perhaps, the end of the beginning."

The USSR

During the latter part of 1941 Hitler made his boldest move to date when he tried to conquer the USSR. Initially, the German forces made great strides, pushing far into the Soviet Union with relative ease. They marched and marched, meeting little if any resistance, but they realized their mistake too late. The country was simply too vast, and despite Russian forces being weak enough to defeat, the bitter cold winters proved too much for the German army. After losses at Kursk and Stalingrad in 1943, the Germans had no choice but to fall back. In 1944 the German forces withdrew from Russia entirely and now it was the Red Army's turn to chase the Germans, which they did, all the way to Berlin.

Despite the Nazi-Soviet Pact of August 1939 Hitler's objective had always been to attack the Soviet Union. Hitler's main ideology included two key objectives: the killing of Jews and lebensraum. He set out to exterminate the Jews because he believed them to be responsible for Germany's defeat in World War I. Lebensraum, or living space, involved obtaining vast domains in the East and the oppression of the Slavic peoples. This was intended to be a war of total destruction, largely because Russia had mostly ignored the Geneva Convention. In Hitler's view this required the implementation of 'executive measures' in any of the lands captured by his troops.

Even when confronted with the vastness of the Russian border, Hitler expected a speedy triumph, so much so that he did not even bother to equip his soldiers with the supplies and winter uniforms so necessary for a Russian Campaign. 'You only have to kick in the door,' said Hitler without hesitation, 'and the whole rotten structure will come down.' Two tons of Iron Crosses were being held in readiness to award those who carried out the destruction of Moscow.

The Soviets' difficult and drawn out war against the Finns proved to Hitler that the Soviets were weak, but he underestimated them by merely measuring them by their past military campaigns. Furthermore, he trusted that the Russian population would welcome his troops, and, to be fair, this is exactly what happened in some places. However, in most of Russia, the invasion by the Nazis was not seen in a positive light at all, and the Germans' ruthless strategies actually alienated the people.

On the 28th of July 1942 Joseph Stalin implemented the 'Not one step back' mandate, this was to ensure the army was driven by fear. Those who tried to flee or showed the slightest indication of cowardice were to be executed immediately. Behind the Soviet lines, there were extra soldiers prepared to shoot any one deemed to be a 'traitor to the Motherland.'

Stalin's spies had long cautioned him about the impending German attack but he did not trust them, so he didn't prepare for the coming invasion. This is why the Germans faced so little resistance when they set Operation Barbarossa in motion at 4 a.m. on the 22nd of June 1941. More than 3 million Axis troops advanced along a 900-mile front into Russia proper.

On that single day one fourth of the Soviet Union's air power was destroyed, and before the end of October, Moscow was just sixty-five miles away and more than 500,000 square miles of the Soviet Union had been overrun. A large number of Soviet troops were murdered and 3 million Red Army soldiers were taken as prisoner. The international war guidelines for the treatment of prisoners were violated because the Germans did not care so much about the rules when it came to Russian troops.

Finland, Hungary and Albania had all declared war on the Soviet Union before the end of June. For Finland, it was a 'sacred war', because it was a chance to seek revenge for the Soviet invasion that had occurred earlier. During this week Stalin went through what was now known to have been a mental breakdown. He vanished into his room and did not give any orders to his officials for some time. When the Politburo came for him, Stalin dreaded it was to replace him with another leader, but the committee only asked him what it was they should do. Stalin addressed his officials on the 3rd of July and gave his famous speech on the 'The Great Patriotic War'.

The German forces were now beginning to slow down because the deeper they struck into Russian territory, the more extended the supply lines became. As Russian forces retreated they pursued a scorched earth policy, where anything of use was destroyed in order to prevent the Germans from using it. Everything was burnt, killed, or spoiled: crops, domesticated animals and shelter. The Russians were in effect holding the front lines by weight of numbers alone: for every ten Russian troops the Germans killed, another ten sprang up to meet them.

Because Germany, Italy and Japan had signed the Tripartite Pact, Stalin was unsure if Japan would aid Germany in attacking Russia. When Stalin learned that Japan intended to honor the previously signed Soviet-Japanese Nonaggression Pact, he was able to redeploy his troops from the Far East to the fight against the Germans. However, it was Russia's most powerful ally 'General Winter' that changed Russia's fortunes. With the onset of pre-winter came the overwhelming downpours, the rain was incessant, so much so that it hampered the German advance, even bringing it to a halt, as vehicles became stuck on poorly maintained and mud caked roads. Hitler had clothed his troops in summer attire, thinking he'd be in Moscow well before the onset of winter. His men did not fare well in the freezing conditions and many became sick as their situation worsened. The morale of the army dissolved as the German soldiers suffered through the winter.

In September German forces had encircled Leningrad and Hitler, instead of bombing it, set out to starve it into submission. Each feline, rodent and living creature was eaten through a paste that was made into soup and then given to the inhabitants. Slowly, all sources of fuel ran out and the city suffered for 872 days until the 27th of January 1944. Roughly 1,000,000 civilians died from stress, starvation and from the lack of fuel that was needed to protect them against the winter. Some supplies got through over Lake Ladoga, but it was not enough for everyone. Some historians note that many inhabitants actually had to resort to eating human flesh to survive.

The Normandy Invasion

In June 1944 the Normandy landings, – or D-Day (Operation Overlord) – was set in motion. It was a day that saw the combined forces of America, Britain and Canada land on the beaches of German-controlled Normandy in an attempt to free Europe from Nazi control. The invasion was successful and the German army was forced to withdraw. Within one year Germany was completely surrounded by the Allied Forces, completely cut off from the rest of the world. In May 1945 Nazi Germany formally surrendered after Hitler committed suicide in Berlin with his mistress.

In the Pacific

Pearl Harbor

For the United States World War II had officially begun in the Pacific on December 7, 1941, when Japanese planes sprang a surprise attack on the American Naval base at Pearl Harbor. Approximately 2400 Americans died in the air raid and more than 1100 others were wounded. With no formal declaration of war from Japan the disbelief of what had happened at Pearl Harbor sent the United States into shock. Stunned by the attack its people were able to find some solace in President Roosevelt's famous, hopeful speech.

For years China and Japan had been locked in a war, with neither side gaining any significant advantage. The Japanese had seized the northern region of Manchuria, which is known today as the Heilongjiang, Liaoning and Jilin provinces. Seeking to expand its territory and secure access to raw materials, such as oil, Japan had launched military campaigns across the Pacific region.

USA and the Battle of Midway

The United States of America officially declared war on Japan the day after the attack. The attack demanded that the military's top brass immediately plunge into strategic planning. The US retaliated several months later, and in 1942, after a succession of naval battles, the Americans finally found themselves victorious in the month of June. The Battle of Midway, a decisive naval confrontation that saw Japan lose four carriers, was theirs.

Guadalcanal and the Solomon Islands

The American and Japanese forces fought for control of the Solomon Islands because they were situated close to important shipping routes used by the Allies. When the Allies invaded Guadalcanal Island, between 1942 and 1943, the Japanese were forced to withdraw because it was too close to the Solomon Islands. At the same time, India and Britain were fighting Japan in Burma, or modern day Myanmar.

Japan

War raged in the Pacific until 1945, with major battles – mainly fought by American forces – seen on Okinawa, Iwo Jima, and Leyte. The majority of those territories that had been seized by Japan were, by this time, freed.

The fighting in the Pacific Theater had been some of the fiercest seen, the Japanese troops were fanatical, ready to die at any cost for their Emperor. The level of fighting was one of the main reasons that the 33rd President of the United States decided not to go ahead with an invasion of the Japanese main islands, but instead opt for something that would change the course of history. Knowing a land invasion would have sacrificed tens of thousands of Americans; President Truman approved the use of nuclear weapons on Japan. Two atomic bombs were dropped on Hiroshima (August 6th) and Nagasaki (August 9th) 1945. The destructive power unleashed by these weapons was so great that Japan surrendered unconditionally soon after.

The Vietnam War

The tensions that brought about the Vietnam War can be traced to various nations, including China and France, both of who played a significant role in the outbreak of hostilities. At the turn of the 20th Century Vietnam had tried to remove French control over the country. Ho Chi Minh, a key organizer of the revolts, established an organization referred to as the Viet Minh.

The First Indochina War

While the Nazis were busy overrunning France during World War II, France had begun to lose control of Vietnam and Japan was able establish a foothold within the country before taking it completely. However, the Japanese met resistance from the Viet Minh who quickly found support in other areas of the country. When Japan surrendered in 1945 the Viet Minh seized Hanoi and declared Vietnam as an independent country. Thus, the Democratic Republic of Vietnam was founded.

However, France did not accept this declaration of independence from the Viet Minh and sent French forces to push the communist rebels back to the north. Ho Chi Minh requested help from America, but the Americans were engaged in the Cold War with the Russians. America was uneasy about giving aid to the communists in Vietnam and supported France instead. The First Indochina War continued between Ho Chi Minh and France until the rebels won at Dien Bien Phu, which forced France to negotiate a treaty with them.

Divided Vietnam

In 1957 Vietnam was officially divided into two nations: South Vietnam and North Vietnam. An emperor, who was supported by France, ruled South Vietnam whereas North Vietnam, according to the Geneva Accords, was under the control of Ho Chi Minh. A temporary DMZ, or demilitarized zone, was established at the 17th parallel to help stop the fighting. A free election, scheduled to run in 1956, was set to reunite the country.

The Cold War

America's stance on the Cold War slowly began to influence events in Vietnam, and ultimately its future. America believed that if North Vietnam fell, it would have a domino effect on all nations within Southeast Asia, bringing vast swathes of humanity under communist rule. America supported Ngo Dinh Diem because he believed in democracy, not communism, and with America's support, he was able to seize power in the south. In 1955 he announced the Republic of Vietnam and cancelled the upcoming elections that had been scheduled for the following year.

The Diem Regime

The new government under Diem soon became corrupt and thus, unsurprisingly, he quickly lost support, so much so that he began to be a figure of hate. Meanwhile the US administration continued to help Diem because the regimes enemies were gaining influence throughout the Republic of South Vietnam. The communist guerrillas, the military arm of the National Liberation Front (NLF), were also known as the

177

Viet Cong. To help Diem a number of military advisors were sent from America to Vietnam to train the South Vietnamese Army, or the ARVN. America's efforts proved in vain, primarily due to the internal political issues surrounding Diem, and the following year America sanctioned an uprising that toppled him as president.

The American Escalation

John F. Kennedy stated that any American involvement would be kept to a minimum; his successor Lyndon B. Johnson had a similar policy. However, this changed when soldiers from North Vietnam attacked American naval ships in 1964. So it was that in 1966 around 400,000 American soldiers were sent to Vietnam.

Quagmire and Attrition

Because the American army was having difficulty progressing into enemy territory, a process known as attrition began, in which the army would try to smother the enemy through a wave of slow destruction. Although there were huge losses at first the Viet Cong's soldiers were clever, because they knew their environment intimately and were able to operate using guerrilla tactics. Disheartened and annoyed, the Americans began to go to further extremes, using Agent Orange and napalm on the enemy, but even these tactics did not deliver the advantage they were so desperate to find.

The Tet Offensive

The Tet Offensive occurred in 1968, when the Viet Cong and the North Vietnamese Army simultaneously launched attacks on almost 30 American sites throughout South Vietnam. Although the American army was able to push the enemy back, the media at home portrayed the attack as devastating for America. As a result, many people withdrew their support for the war in Vietnam. An terribly ugly incident known as the My Lai Massacre also surfaced at this time, this was where a group of soldiers killed and raped between 347 and 504 unarmed mainly women, children and old men, in a little Vietnamese village. Told in newspapers, magazines and on television, many Americans began to even hate their own soldiers.

The Anti-War Movement

In the US a movement that opposed the war in Vietnam began to gain popularity among various sections of society. It slowly gained traction as more Americans joined the movement until it rapidly gained support in 1970, when four students were killed outside Kent State University while protesting. In spite of this, President Nixon declared in a speech that most Americans still supported the war.

Vietnamization and the American Extraction

As more Americans joined the anti-war movement, Nixon promised that he would withdraw American troops from Vietnam and allow South Vietnam to govern itself. Nixon did extract some soldiers, but he also authorized campaigns to bomb the Viet Cong in Laos and Cambodia, even though both of these nations were neutral during the war. Nixon is known to have approved the order without informing Congress, probably because Congress would not have agreed with what he wished to do. When these campaigns were discovered – and with the publishing of the Pentagon Papers in 1971 – President Nixon had no choice but to negotiate an end to the war.

The End of Hostilities and the Collapse of Saigon

Le Duc Tho of North Vietnam and Henry Kissinger of the USA met secretly in 1972 to negotiate a treaty. At the same time, Nixon increased the bombing of North Vietnam so that Le Duc Tho was forced to settle an agreement. In January 1973, they agreed on a ceasefire and the remaining American troops were withdrawn from Vietnam in March 1973.

Although America carried on aiding South Vietnam by providing capital, the funds eventually came to an end. Meanwhile, President Nixon was forced to resign from office due to the Watergate Scandal. In 1975 North Vietnamese forces escalated their attacks and eventually took control of Saigon, which is known as Ho Chi Minh City today. Vietnam, reunified as a communist country, declared itself to be the Socialist Republic of Vietnam and at last the war was over.

Conclusion

Thank you again for purchasing this book.

I hope it helped you learn more about world events from both the distant and not so distant past.

The next step, if I may be so bold to suggest, is to share what you have learned with others. To discuss it, and share opinions, ideas and··· histories!

Finally, if you enjoyed this book, I'd like to ask you a favor. If you would be so kind as to leave a review on Amazon it would be greatly appreciated!

Thank you and... good luck!

Preview of "History of China"

By Adam Brown

Chapter 1: Ancient Chinese Dynasties

Overview of Dynasties

A dynasty, in Chinese literature, refers to a series of rulers from the same family and historical periods named after the family that dominated the country at the time. Some dynasties lasted for many centuries while others were in power for only a few years. The earliest dynasty began with the first ruler in 2200 BC and ended in 1912 with the last Emperor of China. From 1912 to 1949, the country that was previously Imperial China became the Republic of China. Thus, more than 4000 years of dynasties came to an end when the last emperor was forced to leave his seat. From 1949 onwards, the country became known as the People's Republic of China, which continues today.

1: Xia Dynasty (2200 – 1600 BC)

Around 2200 BC, the occupants of what is now Northern China near the Yellow River came under the rule of the Xia Dynasty. There is little evidence for this dynasty's existence apart from some records that were compiled much later by reliable historians. It is theorized that the people began to use bronze during this time due to some evidence suggesting that bronze casting occurred at Erlitou during the Xia Dynasty.

Legend states that it was Yu the Great (2200-2100 BC) who began the dynasty. He was a hard worker among the early settlers who helped to ensure the safety of his people. It is documented that the Yellow River constantly flooded the land and caused great difficulty among the people. Crops would be ruined, homes would flood and the people would complain about the hardship that they were in. Yu the Great is known for building dams that ultimately helped to stop flooding in his community and he became well-known for his nobility, leading to the people choosing him as their ruler. Thus, the very first dynasty was founded. The Xia Dynasty had 17 kings and continued until 1600 BC when the Shang Dynasty came into power.

2: Shang Dynasty (1600 – 1046 BC)

Jie of the Xia Dynasty had begun to oppress the people through taxation and unjust laws that were enacted only to benefit the nobility. The people who suffered the most were peasants, who worked long hours and earned meager wages, and occupied the lower strata of society. Because of the hardship many suffered at the hands of the Xia rule at this time, a rebellion began. People threw their support behind Chen Tang, who convinced them they needed a new king. The revolt spread until Jie, the last Xia emperor, was overthrown by a final battle known as the Battle of Mingtiao. Most of Jie's army either deserted the plain of battle or surrendered to the stronger force of Chen Tang. Thus around 1600 BC, the Shang Dynasty came to power.

Western scholars previously used to debate the existence of the Shang Dynasty because much of the knowledge came only from Ancient Chinese literature. However during the 1920s, archaeological excavations unearthed considerable evidence for its existence. Scholars believe that the Shang Dynasty achieved much more progress than the Xia dynasty but this may be due to the minimal historical data about the Xia Dynasty. Nonetheless, major cities and urban hubs including Anyang and Zhengzhou were established during the Shang Dynasty. At its height, the Shang State only controlled a relatively small area of northern China but their rule became a model for other rival States including the Zhou State.

Manufacturing of bronze is known to have continued during this time period. Brass was made from the abundant suppliers of copper, tin and lead that were dug by the Chinese. The miners provided these metals to blacksmiths, who smelted them into bronze. Most bronze was used for ornaments and for ritual objects while only a small amount was used for weaponry and agriculture.

The Shang organized society in a form of feudalism in which relatives of the king and other nobles were granted land in return for their service and loyalty. This resulted in the kings having a great deal of power, and like the kings before thim, were more at risk of abusing that power. The last Shang king was accused of drunkenness, incest, cannibalism, sadism, and was considered evil. The virtues that had once led to the elevation of the Shang were decimated as a result. Once again, there was an uprising against the tyrant king. Sensing vulnerability, Wu Wang from the east attacked the Shang empire and came to power after winning the Battle of Muye. The defeat of the last Shang king (who ironically had been named King Zhou at his own coronation) in 1046BC effectively began the Zhou Dynasty.

3: The Zhou Dynasty (1046 – 256 BC)

Wu Wang became the first king of the Zhou Dynasty after the Shang fell from power. The dynasty lasted until 256 BC, making it the longest to rule for nearly 800 years. The kings had learned from their predecessors and did not make many of the same mistakes. Wu Wang is known to have established the concept of the "Mandate of Heaven". The people believed that the king was appointed by the divine and only the appointed individual had the right to rule in China. The ancient Egyptian pharoahs had a similar concept in which it was believed the pharoah was the closest to the gods and appointed by the divine.

For Wu Wang, this served two purposes. First, this solidified his claim on the throne as legitimate and unquestionable. He was then not a conquering king but a destined king. Secondly, the mandate quenched any possible dissent with the argument that as a king from the divine, he was the only person fit to rule. This made it more difficult to question the king's ability as ruler, which had led to the previous dynasty's demise. After all, Wang had been sent as the solution to the Shang Emperor, was disgraced by his lack of virtue. The Zhou Dynasty was the third and the last of three Pre-Imperial dynasties.

In the course of the Zhou Dynasty, there were 39 kings who followed one another mostly through father to son succession. Initially, the Zhou Dynasty began well by building a successful defense of the country against the barbarians in the West. However as the centuries passed, the country became disunited and there was a great deal of internal strife. Despite this, there were major advancements in the organization of society, technology, construction, trade and agriculture. Some very important features of Chinese thought and philosophy also came to the forefront during this time, the most notable of which are Confucianism and Tao religion.

In the three pre-Imperial dynasties the ruler was viewed as a king who was both a leader and a warrior. Because he was an intermediary to the divine who resided in heaven, the king would perform rituals with the help of his ministers to speak with his ancestors and the divine. Relics called *Oracle bones* were heated up and the cracks that formed on these bones were interpreted as answers to the questions they asked about the future. Questions inscribed on these bones are among the earliest examples of writing that we have today.

4: The Qin Dynasty (221 – 207 BC)

The Qin Dynasty came to power when Qin Shi Huang defeated the last Zhou king at the Battle of Changping, beginning the First Imperial Dynasty. Shi Huang was the first Emperor of China, because he was the first to successfully control the seven states under his rule. The philosophy of Confucianism was abandoned and replaced with Legalism, which led to a great strengthening and centralization of the state. Shi Huang was a ruthless man who suffered from constant paranoia that others would invade his empire. It was during his reign that the Great Wall of China began construction to protect the outskirts of the empire.

His tomb was surrounded by the statues of the famous Terracotta Army who were meant to fight for the Emperor in the afterlife. Shi Huang had been an unpopular ruler due to his ruthlessness and when he died, the Qin dynasty came to an end. The first emperor is thought to have consumed an elixir that was supposed to grant him eternal life. Instead, it is believed, that elixir is what killed him, and today, scholars believe that he died from mercury poisoning. Nonetheless, through his unification of the seven states, he initiated a chain of rulers that would become known as the Emperors of China.

5: The Han Dynasty (206 BC – 220 AD)

After the death of Qin Shi Huang, the Han Dynasty came to power when the first ruler named himself Emperor Gaozu. Gaozu had come from the lower classes in society and was initially very stubborn in taking advice from his ministers despite their knowledge of the state and how to rule. It is believed he realized the error of his ways when he heard some words of wisdom from his beautiful chamberlain, named Lu Jia, who eventually bore Gaozu a son. The emperor took careful notice of the warning and began to place greater faith in the abilities of his ministers. The Han Dynasty is viewed to be a good dynasty that ruled over a peaceful, wealthy and vast empire. Gaozu gave land and possessions to his relatives and supporters so he could build a strong group of allies. The feudal system was re-established like it had been present during the Zhou era but it slowly diminished as new Han rulers replaced each other over time.

Many power struggles occurred within the families of the emperors because they fathered sons through a number of women. During Gaozu's final years, a bitter fight took place between Lu Jia who had given birth to the Gaozu's favourite son, and the Emperor's favorite, Qi, who had hopes that the succession would go to her own child. Qi's son was the Emperor's preferred heir but when he died in 195 BC, the succession went to Lu Jia's son instead. After the Emperor died, when Lu Jia became the Empress dowager, she began to rule China as regent. When her son died she installed another boy as emperor to maintain her power. However, when the boy grew up, a power struggle began between him and Lu Jia; feeling threatened, she had him replaced as well. She is known to have granted power to her relatives by removing noble families through bloody purges and by giving their estates to her own relatives. Lu Jia remained in power until her death in 180 BC. In the power struggle that followed her death, the family of the Empress dowager was annihilated.

The Han Dynasty went through a time of consolidation, with China expanding southwards and venturing into Vietnam and Korea. The severities of the Qin legal code were steadily reduced so as to make the new status quo popular among the people. The Han Dynasty lasted for over 400 years and were interrupted only once by the brief rebellion and coup of Wang Mang. The dynasty witnessed long periods of prosperity and was notable for advances in the manufacturing of iron, hydraulics and paper. Its influence was so great that the Chinese finally began to see a unified empire as something normal after being divided for hundreds of years. This normalization of the unification benefited the Hans, as the people referred to themselves as the 'Sons of Han' and regarded the Han Empire as a model for the future.

This would change with the fall of the Han Dynasty. The deterioration of the Han Empire can be compared to the decline of the Roman Empire, both of which experienced a long period of power struggles upon their deterioration. After the fall of the Han, there were a total of six dynasties that fought for power during this period in Chinese history, and divided the land once more.

6: The Six Dynasties (220 AD – 589 AD)

The Six Dynasties period of China began from the end of the Han dynasty in 220 A.D. and continued until the rise of the Sui Dynasty in 589 A.D. The dynasties were as follows:

Wu (222-280 AD),

Dong Jin (317 – 420 AD),

Liu-Song (420 - 479 AD),
Nin Qi (479 - 502 AD),

Nan Liang (502-557 AD),
Nan Chen (557-589 AD).

These periods of short rule were marked by struggles between landowners and peasants, between the military and the large number of non-ethnic Chinese who had settled in the North, and between the officials and local rulers. China was divided into what is known as the Three Kingdoms: Wei in the North, Shu in the Southwest and Wu in the South. While the 6 dynasties fought, there was never one Emperor to rule a united China. During the period 317-420, Dong Jin supposedly ruled over a part of China called the 16 Kingdoms, but they were not really under his control. The Chinese have long been fascinated by the personalities, conflicts, and literary works that exist from this period.

The 6 dynasties brought about an age of appalling violence and bloodshed, which is not very different from the last 400 years of European history. However, this period also witnessed a flowering of Chinese literature and some radical cultural changes. The most significant change came with the spread of Buddhism. The religion became an integral part of the Chinese way of life in which Confucianism, Taoism and Buddhist values complemented each other, beginning to construct the rich tapestry that is Chinese ideology and culture today.

7: The Sui Dynasty (581 – 618 AD)

The Sui dynasty began in 581 AD and lasted for 37 years with only 2 emperors. A struggle occurred in Northern Zhou when the Duke of Sui replaced Yuwen Pin as the local ruler. The Duke of Sui is known to have had a mixed ethnicity and he took the name Sui Wengdin when he became Emperor.

Wengdin was a brutal man but he reunited China through highly planned and brilliant military campaigns. During his rule, the Buddhist religion flourished because nearly 4000 temples and pagodas were built with his approval. Clauses that called for prohibitions against both Buddhism and Taoism were also abolished during his reign.

Sui Wengdin was succeeded by his youngest son Sui Yangdin who was notorious for his cruelty and ruthlessness. This ascension to power came about by plotting against his older brother, killing his father, and raping a number of his father's wives. He exploited slaves to build canals and to advance the building projects in China. Unlike his father, however, Sui Yangdin was not a brilliant military strategist, which had been essential for Sui Wengdin to come to power. One of the main things that contributed to the downfall of the dynasty under Sui Yangdin's rule was a series of disastrous military campaigns against the Koreans. This eventually led to Sui Yangdin fleeing after a military defeat, and the fall of the Sui dynasty.

8: The Tang Dynasty (618 – 907 AD)

The first ruler of this Dynasty was a man called Li Yuan who replaced Sui Yangdin, declaring himself emperor and crowning himself a Tang Gaozu. His son, Tang Taizong became the second Tang ruler and is known to have been a brilliant emperor because he was wise enough to take constructive criticism and advice from his ministers. His most trusted advisor, Wei Zhang, helped him to become a noble ruler to the point that he was eventually seen as a saint after his death. Tang Gaozong, the third Tang ruler, is known to have married the famous Empress Wu. When he passed away, she became the only female ruler in Chinese history.

Empress Wu was a capable ruler despite being recorded in a most unfavorable way by the historians of China. Confucianism regarded women as second class citizens and did not allow them to lead the Empire. Empress Wu challenged this view and despite the dissent and sexism, led the country in a more peaceful direction. The century between 650 and 750 AD was a wondrous period of time for the Chinese. The Chinese empire was economically restored through trade with India, Persia, Vietnam, Korea and Japan.

The apex of the Tang period occurred during the reign of Tang Xuanzong, who was in power from 712 to 756 AD. Buddhism continued to flourish in the Tang period and its influence grew among the people. During the Tang Dynasty, the capital city alternated between Chang'an and Luo Yang. The Tang Dynasty continued to push the idea that safeguarding of the borders of the empire was a task best suited to non-Han people. This policy ultimately paved the way for the disasters that came soon afterwards.

At this time, a man named An Lushan of non-Chinese pedigree had made his way into Imperial favor. He had an affair with one of the Emperor's mistresses named Yang Guifei, who was known to be very beautiful. When the Emperor discovered the affair, An Lushan was forced to flee the capital. Because An Lushan felt he had lost honor by fleeing, he raised an army and sacked the capital of Chang'an. This time, the Emperor fled with his mistress Yang Guifei and his chief Minister Yang Guozhong. Both of the Yangs were killed but the Emperor escaped during the flight. An Lushan was not able to take full control and so the Tang Emperor eventually abdicated in favor of his son Tang Suzong. The Tangs regained their capital Chang'an and the core of the empire but their high tide had passed. In the late ninth century, Huang Chao led a campaign against the Tangs and captured the capital of Chang'an, this time managing to keep it. The Tang Dynasty finally came to an end and was followed by a short period of quick succession called the Five Dynasties period.

9: The Five Dynasties (907 – 960 AD)

This was a very short period in the long history of China that covered the years between 907 and 960 A.D. It was a time of much disorder during which China splintered into 10 kingdoms with a total of 40 different rulers. It seems historians remember this era only for the complete political disaster that occurred over the years. However, two significant inventions were made that revolutionized society during this time, and we continue to use them today.

Firstly, a printing press with a movable typing board was invented to write accounts of Chinese ancestors. The bureaucrat Feng Dao is known to have compiled various works using this new technology at the time. He created many biographies in his loyal service to the Five Dynasties but was seen negatively by other biographers. Secondly, the Chinese came up with the idea of using paper money as the main form of currency. It was easy to produce and did not weigh as much as coins that other people in the world were using at the time. As a result, there was a surge in trade and commerce in some of the kingdoms. Because of political strife, the capital was shifted back and forth between Luo Yang and Kaifeng by the rulers. In any case, Chang'an was abandoned and never used again because it had become a city of ruins.

10: The Song Dynasty (960 – 1297 AD)

The first Song emperor was Song Taizu who came to power after the Empire had experienced long periods of political instability. He ruled with the assistance of his generals to control the people until he died in 976 AD. During the Song Dynasty, there was a great flowering of arts in China and an expansion of Confucian philosophy among the working class. The anti-martial ethos of Confucianism came to dominate China and the military allowed much of the power to be distributed among the people so they did not have to intervene in state affairs.

During the reign of the first two emperors, the empire was expanded to push the borders further out again. Initially, the Song Dynasty was centered at Kaifeng in the north and called the Northern Song Dynasty. The center of the empire was transferred to Lin'an in South China after a defeat against the Jin. In 1235, the Song Empire made a terrible mistake by attacking the Mongols who had at that point established themselves as the greatest military power in the world. The Mongols fought back and brought the Song Dynasty to an end.

11: The Yuan Dynasty (1271 – 1368 AD)

Kublai Khan became the ruler of China in 1271 AD and the Emperor in 1279 AD. His name as Emperor was Shizu of Yuan and he founded the first and only non-Chinese dynasty known as the Yuan Dynasty. He moved the capital of China to Beijing, which was not too far from Mongolia. He did this to ensure that his troops did not become "softened" by being stationed in China for so long, as China was seen as militarily "inferior" due to their defeat. The Chinese were forced to pay an extra tax to the Mongols who needed to finance their occupation and expenses. Because of the foreign invasion with no attempt to assimilate with or even appease the Chinese people, Mongol rule was not very popular in China and the people rose up to regain control of their country, achieving independence in 1368.

12: The Ming Dynasty (1368 -1644 AD)
In 1368, Ming Hongwu became the first Chinese Emperor after the Yuan Dynasty was removed from power. He was the first emperor of the Ming Dynasty, which lasted from 1368 to 1644 AD. Ming Hongwu was a bloodthirsty man who did not like the Mandarins and killed thousands of them without any just reason, leading to a decline in popularity and trust. Ming Hongwu's son, Ming Yongle, became the third Ming emperor after he proved himself to be a brilliant soldier. He was obsessed with exploration and expansion of the empire and sent out thousands of soldiers to places near the Indian Ocean, Australia and even to America. Unfortunately, all sea-based expeditions ceased after Yongle died in 1424.

In 1517, the Portuguese arrived and caused significant change, although the Mings did not realize what was happening until it was too late. The Europeans claimed they were visiting only to trade with the Chinese. Initially there was no threat but the responsibilities of the Emperors declined slowly as the Europeans began to influence them. In 1644, the last Ming Emperor hung himself on a hill over Beijing because a rebel leader had successfully seized the city.

13: The Qing Dynasty (1644 – 1912)
The Qing Dynasty was the last imperial dynasty of China and consisted of foreign rulers that were Manchus in origin. Unlike the Mongols, they had adopted Chinese customs and

were mostly regarded as Chinese, leading to a relatively more stable rule. The empire expanded its borders to include the various territories that China controls today. In 1689, the Qings defeated the Russians in the siege of Albazin and took control of the area, but diminished in power when the British arrived. The British sold large amounts of opium to the Chinese and essentially liquidated their economy. Then, they fought a war with them that the Chinese had no chance of winning.

As a consequence, the British were able to establish a strong foothold in China. Empress Cixi came to power and allied herself with some rebels called the Boxers. They declared war on the foreigners but were not successful. In addition, the Chinese had also been invaded by the Japanese in a war prior to fighting the British so they were left severely weakened. The empress died in 1908 and the Qing Dynasty ended in 1911. Thus, the famous dynasties of China that had ruled for over 4000 years finally came to an end.

CPSIA information can be obtained
at www.ICGtesting.com
Printed in the USA
LVHW020618080520
654924LV00006B/566